To Und and James Wurmald
from Robin Fry, the author.

THE
VW BEETLE

THE
VW BEETLE

Robin Fry

DAVID & CHARLES
Newton Abbot   London   North Pomfret (Vt)

British Library Cataloguing in Publication Data

Fry, Robin
    The VW Beetle
    1. Volkswagen automobile
    I. Title
    629.22'22   TL215.V6

    ISBN 0-7153-7859-7

Typesetting by ABM Typographics Ltd.,
Hull and printed in Great Britain by
Biddles Ltd., Guildford, Surrey for
David & Charles (Publishers) Limited
Brunel House   Newton Abbot   Devon

Published in the United States of America
        by David & Charles Inc
North Pomfret   Vermont 05053   USA

Contents

This book is dedicated to my wife Lynda

Introduction

My introduction to the Beetle took place during the late 1950s, when my father, who had always had a weakness for unorthodox vehicles including a 2-cylinder Jowett van and a Heinkel cabin cruiser, decided to widen his experience with one of those rather odd-looking little air-cooled cars from Germany. My own first impressions were not favourable. With sloping contours both fore and aft, it could just as easily appear to be travelling forward when in fact in reverse. Its short front went very much against my more traditional concepts and, as for having an engine at the rear, although far from unique, it just did not seem right. However, it was like moving to a new house which, although strange at first, steadily grows on you, and so the bond of affection between vw owners and their cars is not always fully appreciated by others. The Beetle had a unique shape and sound at the time when many cars, with some exceptions such as the Morris Minor, were just beginning to take on a standard character; that, together with the high quality of its production, attracted such people as my father.

As it turned out, this car proved to be one of the most reliable we had encountered. So much so that it hardly ever saw the inside of a garage. My father was so convinced of its invincibility that he seemed to forget about that vital piece of machinery at the rear. Maybe if the engine had been mounted at the front it might have crossed his mind once in a while, but, in spite of minimal maintenance, the car continued to provide utterly reliable transport up until the early 'seventies and would undoubtedly have continued to do so had it not been for someone running into the back of it while it was stationary. (Mercifully, the car was empty of occupants at the time.)

My first Beetle was a 1962 model and although it had clocked up

100,000 miles, it was still going strong. Like all early Beetles, it could prove tricky on wet roads. It was fitted with cross-ply tyres but after travelling several hundred yards broadside on a pouring wet day these were hastily changed to radials. I also changed the 'candle' lights produced by the inadequate 6-volt system. My current Beetle, a GT model purchased new in 1973, still provides family transport and like my father's early Beetle it has proved completely reliable.

Anyone who has sampled the delights of both older and newer Beetles will be well aware of the vast number of improvements made over the years to the general handling, in the engine sound-proofing in the interior—something instantly noticeable—not to mention the welcome change to 12-volt electrics, which drastically reduces the risk of winding up in a ditch on a foggy night. Later cars of course, like the 1200, have more pep but the days when the Beetle would purr happily along on the lowest octane fuel are sadly but a faint memory for any modern Beetle owner.

My interest in the car's ancestry originated in my schooldays in a liking for motoring history. My collection of old motoring sales catalogues, in particular vw promotional brochures, which I started in the late 'sixties, has enabled me to trace the Beetle as far back as 1949, when Wolfsburg first published catalogues. And the same car is being made today, though no longer available in all countries. Although the 1980 Beetle brochure is glossier and more seductive than those ancient examples, how little the car's appearance has changed over thirty-odd years!

The articles and books on the history of the Beetle that have appeared over the years have tended to concentrate on the background story rather than the technical development of the car. What I have set out to achieve is a straightforward account, informative but not over technical, that concentrates on the vehicle itself without lengthy biographies of the men behind it. I hope that it provides the sort of information that will appeal to Volkswagen owners in general.

Quite a number of facts in this short history have not hitherto been published and the same applies to the photographs which I have chosen on the principle that historical interest should not be sacrificed to picture quality, and I can at least claim that quite a few of them are extremely rare.

Many people have helped me. My thanks go firstly to the Porsche company, in particular, Mr Ghislaine Kaes, the late Professor Porsche's nephew and personal secretary from 1930-51 and now the Porsche company's archivist and historian, for the countless hours spent answering a bombardment of questions over many months. He has also provided numerous photographs, line drawings and copies of early documents which have supplied much little-known information on the pre-war period, and scotched one or two myths which have persisted over the years. As if that kindly and expert assistance was not enough, he read through the final typescript of the book in Thailand when he might have been bathing and seeing the sights of that beautiful country. Such conscientious help certainly went far beyond the calls of duty and friendship.

For chapter 4, covering the period 1945-9, I owe lasting gratitude to Ivan Hirst who was in overall charge of the factory at Wolfsburg during the post-war years of Military Government. Many hours of interviewing and countless telephone conversations have culminated in what is, undoubtedly, thanks to Ivan Hirst, the most authentic account yet of this crucial period in the car's history. Until that excellent British independent vw magazine, *Safer Motoring*, began running a series of articles in the mid-sixties, few people had any idea of the invaluable contribution made by the British in the post-war revival of the Wolfsburg factory, and I'm sure that, like myself, readers will be fascinated by the many recollections of those far-off days provided by Ivan Hirst.

I would also like to thank The Revd Alistair McInnes for providing new information on production figures in the post-war period and also for some extremely rare photographs of the 'specials' built at the factory in 1946.

I am also deeply indebted to the Volkswagen factory in Germany and in particular the chief archivist, Herr Dr Bernd Wiersch, for their enthusiastic support by way of photographs and information.

9

For the British chapter I extend my thanks to James Graydon, managing director of VW GB from 1953 to 1967, for his encouraging interest and for providing information and photographs. I would also like to thank Peter Colborne-Baber and his publicity agent, Francis Clarke, for the John Colborne-Baber story and accompanying illustrations. Last but not least, my acknowledgements go to VW Audi, especially Laura Warren of the public relations department for her generous co-operation in supplying material and for liaison with the Wolfsburg factory.

For the American chapter, I extend my thanks to Volkswagen of America for supplying photographs of advertising and sales statistics.

I would also like to take this opportunity to thank all those others who lent their help and expertise: James and Ute Wormald for translations; Chrysler UK, in particular Mr A. H. Major, senior engineer at the technical library, and Mr Lea-Major, for the kind loan of an original copy of the report by the Humber division produced in 1943 on the Type 82 Kübelwagen; for information on the history of Motor Distributors of Dublin I would like to thank Don Hall Public Relations Ltd, Malahide, County Dublin; and lastly, my thanks go to Bob Shaill of the Split Rear Window Club of Great Britain for numerous copies of articles and photographs, and also to Jim McLachlan, founder of the international Volkswagen model club, for photographs and information.

If at First you Don't Succeed . . .

In December 1935, two strange vehicles made their way through the narrow, twisting roads of the Black Forest in Germany. Despite their spartan appearance, these first two Volkswagen prototypes, even at this early stage of development, already had the familiar lines of the Beetle, lines which were to remain basically unaltered for decades. These early Beetles marked the opening of one of the most interesting chapters in motoring history. The man behind it all was Ferdinand Porsche.

Displaying a striking resemblance to the Beetle we know today, these first Volkswagen prototypes, the V1 and V2, are seen here on a day out with the Porsche family in the Black Forest.

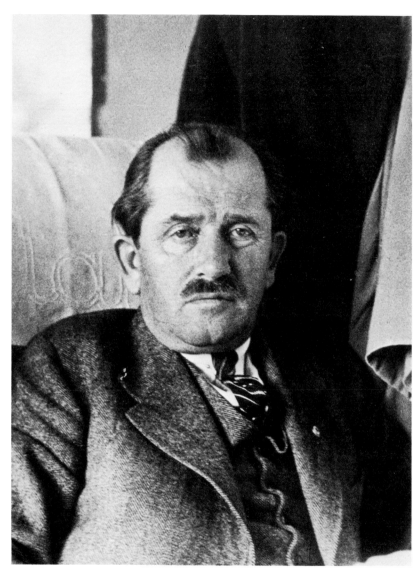

The man behind it all, Ferdinand Porsche.

Porsche, who was born in 1875 in Austria, the son of a tinsmith, had developed a special interest early in his career in finding the best way to transmit power from engine to driving wheels, something which was to have an influence on his future rear-engine designs. It also led to his unorthodox approach to the Porsche Lohner Chaise battery-operated car, his earliest achievement, built in 1897 while he was at the Jacob Lohner Company in Vienna, as their chief automotive designer. It employed a system of hub-mounted electric motors that was a complete departure from the more conventional layout of a centrally mounted, single electric motor, connected to the drive wheels by belts, chains and gears. This novel car was shown at the Paris World Fair of 1900, where it attracted the interest of the motoring public and earned international recognition for its designer almost overnight. To improve the car's performance, Porsche had replaced the heavily loaded batteries with a petrol-driven generator. The design also did away with the need for a gearbox—which in those days, with no syncromesh, made driving an arduous and noisy affair—and the car enjoyed considerable popularity in the early 1900s.

In 1900 Porsche designed and built an electrically driven racing car with batteries weighing 35.4cwt (1,800kg). It was a private deal, for an Englishman, and Porsche delivered the car himself (a visit which left him a confirmed Anglophile).

In 1906 Porsche, now an established designer and engineer was invited to become the technical director of Austrian Daimler in Wiener Neustadt (which became Austro Daimler in 1910 by appointment to the Emperor Franz Joseph I, who granted permission to the company to use the Imperial Arms). One of the new technical director's first tasks was the reorganisation and extension of the rather antiquated workshops and the improvement of working conditions. He modified a number of their existing designs and produced a lorry for the military. As technical director, Porsche liked to supervise personally all projects throughout their development, conferring with his staff and discussing technical matters in great detail, although this kind of activity by a senior member of staff was frowned upon by the conservative management.

One of Porsche's notable successes in those days was the development of a sports car christened the 'Maja' which won success in motoring events, and in 1909 he designed an entirely new car fitted with a 90hp engine for entry in the 1910 Prince Henry Trials. These Trials were a seven-day endurance run, and all three Porsche cars completed the course, with an outright win for the company. Although these cars ran some 16kph (10mph) faster than their nearest rivals, they were deliberately never pushed to the full, as Porsche believed that power units should always work well within their limits.

In 1909 flying machines powered by unreliable French engines were being flown from a field just outside Wiener Neustadt in an area ideally suited because of its flat terrain. Porsche, a keen spectator of this unusual sight, felt as a designer that much could be done to improve the safety of aviation by way of more efficient aero engines. This led to the inauguration of an aero-engine department at the Daimler Motor Company in 1909, where a new 100hp water-cooled engine was developed and supplied to the Austrian armed forces for use in airships. In 1912 Porsche introduced a new range of lightweight air-cooled aero-engines, with a 4-cylinder, horizontally opposed layout and overhead pushrod valves, a specification which foreshadowed the vw engine.

Vehicles of war were now to take priority in the designer's activity, and particularly those with aero-engines, for by 1911 the clouds of war were already gathering over Europe. Porsche was not as yet to be able to pursue his ideal of a car that was smaller and more efficient than the heavy cumbersome vehicles around at the time.

His inventiveness and ability to produce designs often of a highly unorthodox nature seemed almost limitless. One classic example of his ingenuity was a vehicle to transport a giant howitzer, consisting of a train of six units. This was a design which he had begun in 1912, when the company began manufacturing an even longer train consisting of ten tractor units. Each of these were fitted with electric hub motors, the power being supplied from a petrol-driven generator at the head of the train. This snake-like monster could be used for a variety of purposes, such as a troop or supply carrier, and its wheels could be changed to enable it to travel by road or rail.

In 1917 Porsche was made managing director of Austro Daimler.

14

The same year he received even higher recognition for his invaluable contribution to the war effort, when he received an honorary doctorate in engineering from the Vienna Technical University, and was henceforth known as Dr Porsche.

After the war, Porsche began to give serious consideration to the design possibilities of a small, cheap car. This of course was not an entirely new idea to him by any means for, as early as 1901, he had designed and built for a gentleman by the name of Rudolf von Gutmann a Voiturette which featured his electric hub motors with four-wheel brakes. It was delivered on 1 May of that year. Porsche's second attempt had come in 1909, this being a 4-cylinder, 2-litre-engine car developing 18hp which, according to a contemporary article, had tremendous acceleration. In the autumn of 1909 Porsche had driven this car from Wiener Neustadt to London and back without encountering any trouble whatsoever, quite an achievement for the time!

Porsche's keen interest in small cars led to a number of discussions with his friend and designer, Hans Ledwinka of the Czechoslovakian firm of Tatra, in which they exchanged ideas on small-car designs. Ledwinka's plans included a 2-cylinder, air-cooled engine fitted at the front, with central-tube chassis. These innovations were to feature prominently in Porsche's small-car activities some years later, and led up to the vw design. Porsche and Ledwinka were also among the few designers of the day with such advanced ideas as independent wheel suspension and central-tube chassis.

The war had left its mark, and Dr Porsche found himself working in a greatly diminished Austria. War had left that country, like the majority of Europe, in a state of financial ruin, and the average working man considered himself lucky if he could afford a new pedal cycle, let alone a car. The middle classes were little better off in this respect and certainly could not afford the type of vehicle that Austro Daimler had been making. A few manufacturers, however, had woken up to reality. Citroën of France had introduced the '5cv'—a small, economical car which was to prove highly successful. In England, Herbert Austin, later

15

to become Lord Austin of Longbridge, had been thinking along similar lines with his 750cc Austin 7, which survived well into the 1930s. Porsche was a great admirer of Henry Ford, the pioneer of mass production in the United States, and his Model T was achieving the success the Beetle was to achieve and surpass in Germany after World War II. This was to prove an inspiration to Porsche, who had similar ideas for a car within the financial reach of ordinary working individuals.

It would, however, seem unlikely that he would have had the working class in mind at that time, as vehicle ownership would certainly have been outside their financial scope, no matter how cheap the cars were. The middle classes would have seemed a more likely target, although not all of them could have afforded a new car by any stretch of the imagination. Since 1918 Daimler had stuck exclusively to the luxury end of the market, and were convinced that their well-established reputation would be sufficient to sell such vehicles in the post-war market. Porsche designed a number of these luxury carriages. 1920 saw the introduction of a 6-cylinder, $4\frac{1}{2}$-litre car known as the 'AD 617', followed by several similarly large vehicles, some with slightly smaller power units, but nevertheless transport for the moneyed classes.

One further opportunity arose for Porsche to develop a small car whilst with Daimler, when one of his influential friends, Count Kolowrat, expressed a desire for a small sports car. The Count, a film magnate, was so keen on the idea, that he was prepared to finance the development of such a car. The arrangement was accepted by Austro Daimler's management and a small, lightweight 1.1-litre sports car, nicknamed the 'Sascha' by the Count, was developed. The racing version of it proved a roaring success. In 1922 a team of Saschas were entered in the Targa Florio in Sicily, taking first and second place. They went on to achieve numerous other successes—fifty-one firsts in all— including wins in Austria, the Netherlands, Spain and Hungary, and in England at Brooklands, Southend, Shelsley Walsh and Porthcal.

1923 was to see the end of Porsche's career with Austro Daimler. The story that led up to this resignation concerned Austro's main shareholder, Camillo Castiglioni, a businessman and stock-exchange gambler, who asked Porsche to make redundant one third of the workforce—

16

about 2,000 in all—so that Austro Daimler's shares on the Dutch stock exchange would drop in price. He also asked Porsche to hand over all foreign currencies he was holding to be exchanged for Austrian currency, at a time when Austria, like Germany, was suffering from raging inflation. Porsche refused to be a party to this sort of activity and was made redundant.

In February 1923 Porsche left his native Austria and headed for Stuttgart in the state of Württemberg in southern Germany where on 30 April he signed a five-year contract making him technical director and member of the board at Daimler Motoren. (Later, in 1926, due to their worsening financial position, Benz & Cie of Mannheim were forced to merge with Daimler and the name was changed to Daimler-Benz.) He went to live at 48-50 Feurbacherweg, overlooking Stuttgart, which was to serve as a permanent residence and still remains in the Porsche family today. Porsche's move to Germany and a people known for their reserve was not helped by a letter received from the government, informing him that his honorary degree could not be recognised in Germany. However, Porsche's reaction to this was to come in the form of a racing car.

Although he was still to pursue his small-car ideals, his term of office with the new company was to be marked in the early years with vehicles whose engine capacities lay at the opposite end of the scale, in a series of high-performance cars—the mighty Mercedes. First came the development of a supercharged, 8-cylinder, 2-litre car which made its racing début in 1924 at Monza where three cars were entered, but were withdrawn after a certain Count Zborowski (of Chitty Bang Bang fame) drove to his death in one of them. In the meantime, Porsche had developed a supercharged, 6-cylinder, touring car, along with a supercharged version of an Austro-Daimler 4-cylinder, 2-litre model which, in the hands of racing driver Christian Werner, won outright at the 1924 Targa Florio. In recognition of this last achievement Porsche was, ironically, awarded an honorary doctorate in engineering by the Württemberg Technical High School in Stuttgart.

In 1926, Rudolf Caracciola, driving one of Porsche's 8-cylinder, 2-litre cars, took the record on the track at Berlin with an average speed of 82.3mph (135.2kph). The following year heralded the model 'K' ('Kompressor-supercharger'), with a 6-cylinder, supercharged, 6200cc power unit, last of the Daimler cars before the merger. The K model was followed by the mighty 'S' ('Sports'), with a 6789cc engine, and in 1928 the 'SS' ('Super Sports'), 7100cc, which, when supercharged, could attain 225bhp, and finally in 1928 the 'SSK' ('Kurz, short chassis') and the 'SSKL', capable of 225bhp and 250bhp respectively whilst engaging their outsized superchargers, limited to short duration for fear of engine catastrophe.

The Austrian designer who, a few years previously, had entered Germany quietly and alone, had by now established himself and won fame for a series of sports cars which, in the hands of famous racing drivers such as Caracciola and Christian Werner, had notched up a formidable number of victories both in Germany and abroad.

Porsche now turned his thoughts once more to small cars and in 1926 he introduced a 6-cylinder, 2-litre model, the 8/38, called rather appropriately the 'Stuttgart'. However, this proved to be something of a headache to its designer as it was reluctant to start in cold weather—a problem created by perforated cylinder castings.

In 1928 Porsche came nearer to achieving one of his greatest ambitions with a new model, with development number 130, fitted with a 1280cc, 4-cylinder, water-cooled, front engine, developing 25bhp at 3,300rpm and with a maximum speed of just above 52mph (84kph) and independent wheel suspension. The car proved sufficiently successful to justify a series of thirty prototypes which were, in fact, road tested. However, Porsche found himself up against strong opposition from members of the board to his plans to market a small vehicle, particularly those formerly from Benz who did not wish Daimler-Benz to be associated with a vehicle destined for purchase by the middle class. There were continual disagreements, made worse by the failure of the Stuttgart, which the Benz management seized upon in their attempt to over-ride Porsche. The situation eventually reached a climax and Porsche, who could no longer tolerate the attitude of the members of the board, was made to resign.

He moved back to Austria where he took up the position of technical director, chief engineer and member of the board at Steyr Werke of Steyer, Austria. One of the first creations by Porsche to bear the company's name was the Steyr XXX which was fitted with an engine bearing a close resemblance to the power unit developed for the ill-fated Stuttgart. The new car, however, proved highly successful and remained in production for a number of years. The Steyr XXX was followed by a model called the 'Austria', powered by a 5.3-litre, 8-cylinder engine. This car, of considerably advanced design, featured such items as dual ignition, overdrive and a lubrication system limited to a single grade of oil. The Austria proved a star attraction at the 1929 Paris Motor Show, adding another success to Porsche's career.

Unfortunately, at the same time as Steyr were enjoying the successful début of this latest vehicle, they were faced with a sudden crisis created by the collapse of one of Austria's leading banks, the Österreichische Bodenkreditanstalt, which held major shares in the company, following the Wall Street collapse. This led to the industrial assets of Steyr being acquired by another major banking concern, Kreditanstalt Am Hof, which had amongst its assets Porsche's old company, Austro Daimler, who, of course, would not even consider having Porsche on the board. The famous designer found himself once again out of work—and it was now the beginning of the Depression.

2

First Steps

In 1930 Porsche returned to Stuttgart and in December set up in business at 24 Kronenstrasse under his own name as 'Dr Ing. hc Ferdinand Porsche GmbH Designer and Consultant for Engines and Vehicles'. A factor in Porsche's decision to set up business in Stuttgart was the specialist skills in the area, with such firms as Bosch, Mahle, Behr and Hirth, the famous Stuttgart Automotive Research Centre and the Stuttgart Technical University.

Karl Rabe, who had worked under Porsche at Austro Daimler and Steyr, soon joined him as chief designer. Other recruits were Josef Kales (specialist in engines), Karl Fröhlich (gear boxes), Josef Zahradnick (axles and steering) and Erwin Komenda (body designs). All were Austrians and most of them had worked with Porsche before. Although he was not able to offer his staff competitive wages they were only too eager to work under their old master because they had complete trust in him and wanted to share in the sort of exciting opportunities they were unlikely to get elsewhere, under a more conservative management. Capital for the new company was put up by its first finance director, Adolf Rosenberger, a businessman and friend of Porsche's who had been a racing driver for Mercedes. Rosenberger was a Jew and he had to leave the country in 1933. He was kept on as the company's representative in Paris where he marketed Porsche's torsion-bar designs until the outbreak of World War II, when he headed for the States. He was replaced by Johann Kern who joined Porsche along with Hans Baron Veyder-Malberg. Malberg later became Porsche's liaison man with the Nazi hierarchy. Amongst other members to be there right at the beginning were Dr Porsche's driver and general factotum, Josef Goldinger, who had been with him since 1908, his nephew, who became his private secretary, Ghislaine Kaes and Franz Sieberer, who was to be in charge of copying the original drawings. Porsche was also joined by his son, Ferry, who had completed his apprenticeship with Robert Bosch Electric at Stuttgart. Many of these original staff members were to remain with the company until their retirement. (The company, under the same name, runs today with a staff of 6,000 and is one of the world's leading design consultants and sports-car manufacturers.)

One of the first tasks undertaken by Porsche on his return to Stuttgart was a car design for the Wanderer company of Chemnitz (now Karl-Marx-Stadt) with a 6-cylinder, in-line engine of 1692cc developing 35bhp, also available with a 2-litre engine developing 40bhp. These models were later followed by an 8-cylinder version with a $3\frac{1}{2}$-litre engine, also available with a supercharger. One of the 8-cylinder cars was fitted with streamlined bodywork, but this final project had to be abandoned in 1932 when the Wanderer company became part of the new consortium, Auto Union. The streamlined prototype was retained by Porsche for personal use.

Having established himself in Stuttgart, Porsche turned his thoughts once more to small-car designs. The work schedule, made up of a variety of projects arranged in numerical order began at 7; 8 and 9 were the car-design work for the Wanderer company, whilst 10 was a vehicle with a rear, swing-axle design for the Horch company of Zwickau in Saxony, who also became part of Auto Union. Project 12 was to be devoted to the initial designs of a small car.

Many would have considered the idea of bringing motoring to those unable to afford the luxury of four-wheeled transport as wishful thinking at a time when unemployment was still high, and in many respects little had changed since the early 'twenties when Porsche had tried to persuade Austro Daimler to move in the same direction. Porsche may have felt, however, that the economy must eventually turn the corner and that the market would then be open to those ready to provide the right kind of vehicles. In the meantime his small car would at least satisfy the needs of some people. Certainly there was a lesson to be learnt from those less fortunate manufacturers of prestige cars and, for that matter, more moderately priced vehicles, many of whom had established their

21

businesses well before World War I but had since faded into oblivion. Although small cars were no strangers to the German motoring scene and a number of models were available at that time, Porsche viewed many of these as totally inadequate. To him a small car should be designed specifically as such and not be just a scaled-down compromise of a larger vehicle. His car would be designed from scratch with a completely unorthodox approach, and would have to be capable of good performance in reasonable comfort with the utmost degree of economy and reliability.

With these thoughts in mind, Porsche and his chief designer, Karl Rabe, met on 13 September 1931 and poured over designs for a people's car. The aerodynamic shape of the car they were planning was unusual to say the least, and certainly bore little resemblance to the more conventional vehicles on the market. It featured a back which sloped away to give a humped-back appearance—more akin to a bug than a car —plus a high rear window, despite which the car had surprising good rear vision. The engine was to be situated at the back, which would eliminate the need for a drive shaft connecting the gear box to the differential, thus avoiding the torque load this imposed. The engine was to be located just aft of the rear axle, with an integrated, 4-speed gearbox and differential unit to the fore of the rear axle. The increased weight over the back wheels would have the added benefit of improved traction, a useful feature on snow-clad roads and rough terrain.

In order to equal the smooth ride of more expensive vehicles, Porsche opted for a novel form of independent wheel suspension with a swing axle at the rear. The two-door body, which would take the form on the production model of a steel shell made up from a number of individual pressings, could be mass-produced more quickly and cheaply than the traditional wooden frame covered with steel sheeting or cloth fabric. Further weight reduction would be achieved by the use of a central backbone frame in place of the more normal heavy cross-member chassis. No final decision had been taken as to the type of power unit, but a 3-cylinder radial seemed most likely.

This then was the outline of Porsche's masterplan for the small car of the future as described to Rabe on that September day. The finer technical details could be interpreted by each member of the team with their specialist knowledge. It was certainly an exciting challenge to all of them as the design and location of even the smallest component was to be analysed in great detail. Still only a dream on paper, Project 12 was to lay the foundation of Porsche's people's car.

Although Porsche's own design work was to play a major part in the creation of Project 12, some of the principles involved had already been used by pioneers such as Ledwinka with the famous Tatrichek. This had an air-cooled, 2-cylinder boxermotor located at the front, with a central-tube backbone frame, and swing axles at the rear. Whereas the central member on the Czechoslovakian car was actually a steel tube connecting front to rear, Porsche's design had a box-profile backbone frame. Attempts at streamlining go back as early as 1899 with Jenatzy's 'La Jamais Contente' which featured a body also made up from sheet-metal panels. Electrically propelled, this car took the land speed record with a speed of 65.9mph (106kph). Since that time, numerous designers had contrived to reduce wind resistance by the use of streamlining. One classic example worthy of mention, was that of the Benz 'Tropfenwagen', a design built under licence from Dr Edmund Rumpler, who also, incidentally, took out a patent on Germany's earliest swing-axle design, way back in 1903—for an Adler car. Featuring the famous aerodynami-cally shaped 'Teardrop body' the Tropfenwagen, fitted with swinging rear axles and a 6-cylinder radial at the rear, gave a highly creditable performance. The design disappeared with the merger with Daimler in 1926. One of the most intriguing of all was a drawing by a Jewish student called Bela Barenyi. This featured a central backbone chassis, independent wheel suspension and a horizontally opposed, air-cooled engine at the rear, with an enclosed cooling system. In fact, it was almost a blueprint of the Volkswagen. However, it was Porsche's own fanatical addiction to the small-car ideal and the expertise of his design team which brought so many design concepts into one major scheme and eventually heralded in the greatest small car of all.

Now it was a question of evolving test-bed vehicles to try out the new small-car plan. The timing, however, could not have been less fortunate, Germany being still in a state of deep depression with few prospects of

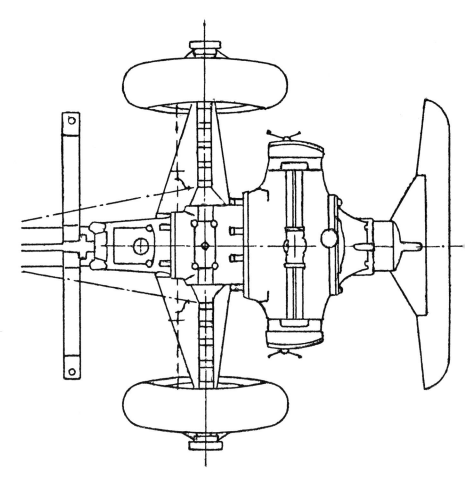

The sketch made in 1926 by the Hungarian Jewish student, Bela Barenyi, which foreshadowed the later design for the Volkswagen. It includes a central-tube backbone frame, independent wheel suspension, the boxermotor and an enclosed cooling system.

immediate recovery. The motor industry, whose merchandise to a greater extent came under the heading of luxury goods, was particularly hard hit and not really in a position to gamble their dwindling funds on new enterprises. Most had to make do with current lines, saleable or otherwise, as they lacked the necessary capital needed for further development. Those who could raise the cash, would have been unlikely to consider anything as unconventional as Project 12. There was one exception, however— Dr Fritz Neumeyer, proprietor of the Zündapp motorcycle company and an industrialist with a number of business interests in and around Nürnberg. He had started building motorcycles just after World War I and within a few years had created one of the largest motorcycle industries in Germany. His interest in small cars dated back to the mid-1920s when he imported two small Rovers from England with a view to building the model under licence in one of his own factories. Neumeyer, of course, was in a similar situation to his competititors, but he adopted the attitude that, if he could not sell current stock—and the motorcycle industry which supplied transport for the working classes was amongst those hardest hit, then an alternative would have to be found. Neumeyer approached Porsche and it turned out that his ideas ran fairly parallel with those of Porsche. There were, however, differences in the type of power unit to be employed. Neumeyer favoured a 5-cylinder, water-cooled radial as he felt that an air-cooled engine would be too noisy in a car. Porsche on this occasion was in no position to argue, and readily conceded, considering himself fortunate to have found someone willing to provide the necessary funds to breathe life into his new creation.

The contract which followed their meeting at Kronenstrasse outlined a small, two-door car powered by a 1200cc engine, returning a fuel consumption of 35mpg (12.4km per litre), with a top speed somewhere in the region of 60mph (96kph). Three prototypes were to be constructed for the purposes of evaluation and testing—two saloons and a cabriolet— one of which would be retained by Porsche for his personal use. He would also receive full remuneration for future development costs, and an amount towards those incurred to date, being one third to begin, one third on delivery, and one third from sales. The contract work for

The 1931 Zündapp Type 12, which featured a lightweight, central box member frame, a 5-cylinder water-cooled radial engine and independent wheel suspension—the latter a special design by Porsche.

A study in aerodynamics, undertaken with the Zündapp. Bodywork was by Reutter. This was developed from blueprints used for an earlier project with the Wanderer company. The simple body lines with integral headlamps and sloping rear were to become permanent features in future developments with the Volkswagen company. The location of the engine is revealed by the louvres behind the rear passengers' window.

the prototype bodies was undertaken by the well-known Stuttgart firm of Reutter. The construction work, which was to be carried out in the utmost secrecy to prevent other enterprising individuals entertaining similar ideas, would be carried out under Porsche's personal supervision and would involve a special night shift, employing selected craftsmen from Reutter's staff. In order to ease construction of the prototypes and save time and costs, the bodies were built from aluminium wrapped around a wooden frame.

By April 1932 the bodies were completed and transported to Nürnberg for final assembly with the engines and chassis which had been built at the Zündapp works. The bodywork of the Zündapps, evolved from revised versions of blueprints used in the development of the 3.2-litre, streamlined Wanderer, looked in many respects like a scaled-down version of its aerodynamically shaped predecessor, and certainly showed several similarities to the earlier prototype. Like the Wanderer, headlamps were integrated into the wings, a fashion at that time (along with enclosed rear wheel-arches, and a sloping rear-end akin to the later Beetle). The secret of the car's rear-engine location was revealed by louvres behind the rear passengers' side-windows. To accommodate the power unit in the rather confined space created by the sloping contours of the rear, the engine had to be mounted in a slightly forward-tilted position to clear the engine hatch.

Independent wheel suspension was achieved at the front by a transverse, 3-leaf spring, mounted centrally to the box-member frame and connected by means of eyes and bolts to radius-arms. These carried end-mounted, friction-type shock-absorbers and the stub axles, with the shock-absorber levers anchored to a transverse member at the head of the frame. This also carried the steering gear. The opposite ends of the long radius-arms were mounted either side in bearings inside the central-frame member where they appear to have been connected via a swivel-joint. vw-type swinging half-axles were employed at the rear, with a centrally mounted, four-leaf spring. The rear wheels were located by long trailing arms hinged to the box-chassis side-members. In order to cope with the extra weight of the engine, the central member was located at the rear by a cross-brace which ran under the power unit and was located to the half-axle casings on either side.

Brakes were hydraulic, but mechanical brakes were to be offered as an alternative on the production model. Electrics were by Bosch of Stuttgart. The 5-cylinder radial fitted with a Zenith carburettor developed 26bhp at 3000rpms with a top speed of 50mph (80.5kph) under test. The fourth gear was in the later tradition of the vw and allowed the car to cruise at a relatively high speed without over-revving the engine. Overall length was 10.9ft (3,330mm), breadth was 4.7ft (1,420mm) and height 4.9ft (1,500mm), with a maximum weight, including four passengers, of approximately 17.7cwt (900kg).

Early road-tests were to prove a nightmare, with two of the cars grinding to a sudden halt after covering little more than a few miles of their maiden journey because the multi-barrelled radials had seized up completely. Attempts were made to remedy the problem by modifying the cooling system to lower the extreme temperatures responsible for the alarming failure. After this initial delay, the cars ventured forth once more, only to experience further problems, this time attributable to the transmission, when gear teeth began snapping off.

Having sorted out these early failures, the cars began a series of longer-distance, high-speed runs, where they behaved reasonably well. But once again, Porsche's ambitions were to be thwarted, for Neumeyer decided to abandon the project. One of the reasons for this change of mind was the sudden, unexpected upturn in motorcycle sales. Another major factor was the high cost of the large presses required to produce the all-steel body, plus the numerous problems which plagued the cars during the early part of the test programme. All in all, the situation left Neumeyer feeling a lot less optimistic over the commercial viability of Porsche's new creation.

The three little Zündapp cars continued in existence for a number of years only to be destroyed in two separate bombing incidents during World War II.

Incidentally, the name 'Volksauto', which Neumeyer was reported to have used when referring to the Zündapp car project, was never in

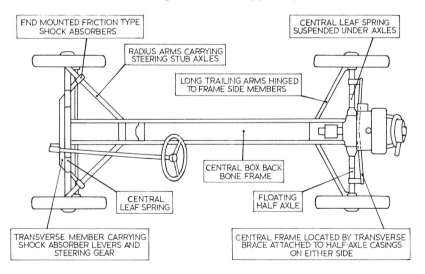

A drawing made in 1932 for the Zündapp Type 12, showing the evolution of the Volkswagen's central-tube backbone platform frame and independent wheel suspension.

fact, as Ghislaine Kaes has pointed out, used as an official designation for these or the next prototypes developed by Porsche for the NSU company, contrary to the myth which seems to have stemmed from early accounts and has been adopted by various authors ever since.

It was about mid-1932, when the Zündapp project was well in hand, that Porsche began receiving letters from Russia, followed by a visit from a small Russian delegation who showed considerable interest in his work. After discussions on a wide range of technical matters, he was given an invitation to visit the Soviet Union to see for himself the progress which had been made since the Communist takeover. The proposals made to Porsche by the Russians lay beyond his wildest dreams, with offers of all possible facilities, plus financial remuneration far beyond anything he could ever hope to achieve in Germany or elsewhere. He was invited on a conducted tour of the country to see what would lie in store should he accept this posting.

His stay in Russia lasted almost a month and he travelled thousands of miles visiting a wide cross-section of Russian industry. Further tempting offers were also forthcoming, allowing Porsche not only to bring his family but also the staff of his chosing, all of whom would be offered luxury accommodation. In fact nothing seemed to be too much trouble if it would persuade this eminent designer and engineer to give up his business interests in Germany and opt for a new life in Russia. Despite the problems he faced back home, and the fact that things were not going too well financially, Porsche turned down the offer, for he realised that, at the age of fifty-four, he would be unable to master the language sufficiently to allow him to make any headway in a posting where he would have to be capable of fluent Russian speech in order to deal with technical matters. Porsche was obviously highly impressed by what he had seen and said to Ghislaine Kaes, 'I never expected the Communists to be this clever'.

However, even before the Zündapp project had been concluded, Porsche had received another small-car client at Kronenstrasse, this time Baron Fritz von Falkenhayn, managing director of the NSU Motorcycle Company at Neckarsulm. As it turned out, NSU had been thinking, along similar lines to Zündapp, that a small, cheap, four-wheeled vehicle could prove a useful addition to their range, particularly at a time when motorcycle sales were down. NSU had previously been in the car business in a joint venture with Fiat of Italy, before selling out to Fiat in 1930 (under an agreement not to manufacture cars in the future— something which seems initially to have been overlooked).

The first discussions between the two parties took place at Porsche's office in the summer of 1933, during which Porsche voiced his intentions of replacing the rather troublesome radial unit used in the Zündapp design with an air-cooled unit. This design went back to Daimler days when, in 1912, he had designed a 4-cylinder, horizontally opposed layout, with overhead valves which had proved so successful in aircraft, known in Germany as the 'boxermotor'. This idea appealed to von Falkenhayn, as an air-cooled engine would not only prove cheaper to manufacture, but would also enable them to utilise their own experience with motorcycle engines. Three prototypes were to be manufactured, under a contract drawn up between NSU and Porsche, and the project was listed number 32. Although a continuation of the work carried out under Project 12, Project 32 with the NSU was to lay many of the foundation stones in the future development of the Volkswagen. First drawings for the new design were completed on 2 August 1933.

The 4-cylinder, horizontally opposed, air-cooled engine for the NSU has been attributed to the work of Josef Kales. However, the development of the NSU engine has in the past been a subject of some controversy. This revolves around an Englishman, Walter Henry Moore, at that time working as chief designer for the NSU company at Neckarsulm. Moore had worked as chief designer for the Norton motorcycle company in England, before joining NSU about 1930.

Moore claimed that when he visited the office at Kronenstrasse he found little in the way of completed designwork on the proposed engine, but that Porsche had fairly detailed outlines and sketches of the cylinder layout which, in Moore's opinion, would be utterly impracticable. Whereas with the VW engine each pair of opposed cylinders are offset, in the Porsche layout they were directly in line with one another, using only two crankpins. This made it impossible to use direct-thrust conrods as, theoretically, they would be mounted at precisely the same point

31

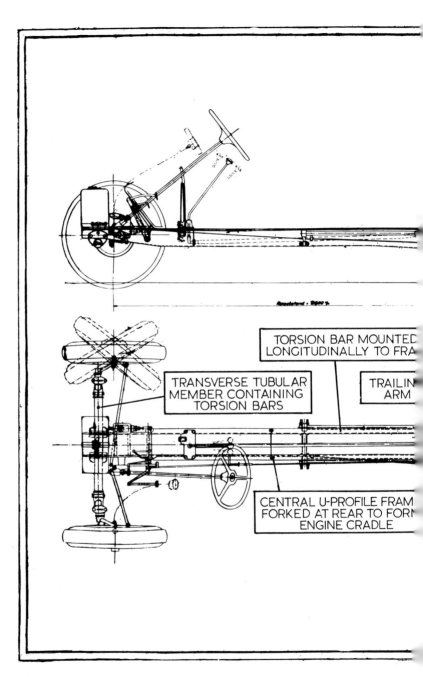

TORSION BAR MOUNTEC
LONGITUDINALLY TO FRA

TRANSVERSE TUBULAR
MEMBER CONTAINING
TORSION BARS

TRAILIN
ARM

CENTRAL U-PROFILE FRAM
FORKED AT REAR TO FOR
ENGINE CRADLE

A drawing made in 1933 for the NSU Type 32.

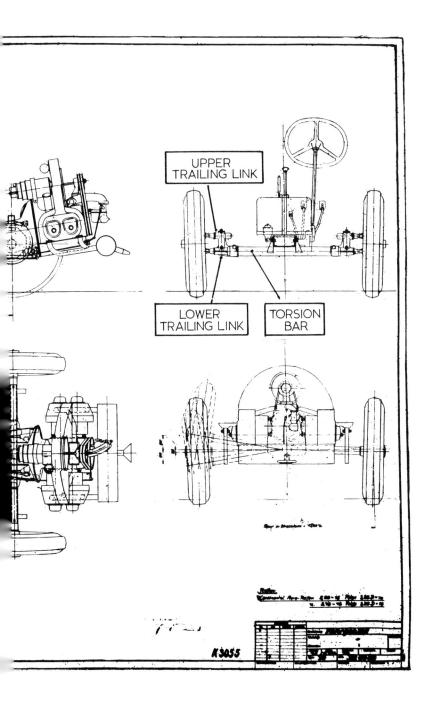

UPPER
TRAILING LINK

LOWER
TRAILING LINK

TORSION
BAR

K3055

on the crankpin. To overcome this, Moore claims, the con-rods were inclined and, as they now lay on the slant, this ruled out the use of conventional small- and big-end bearings. Instead, these were spherical with the big ends mounted in spherical seatings which were clamped in the con-rods, with spherical small-end bearings. This rather bizarre design, Moore felt, was doomed from the outset as the side stresses imposed on both con-rods and cylinders would prove intolerable.

Moore claims that he rearranged the cylinders to their present position. This meant lengthening the crankshaft slightly so that each pair of opposed cylinders were staggered in an offset position—as on the Volkswagen engine—with the con-rods mounted side by side on a single crankpin either side of a two-throw crankshaft. A sketch of this arrangement appeared in *Autocar* 9 July 1943.

Moore then went on to say that, on the original design, the camshaft was placed on top of the crankcase, with the valve gear on the top side of the horizontal cylinders—a layout which, in Moore's experience, created lubrication problems. As well as starvation of the rocker gear, excess oil tended to find its way into the cylinders via the rocker boxes and the inlet-valve guides. Instead, Moore says, he placed the camshaft below the crankshaft, which kept it immersed in oil and, as the slightly inclined valve push-rod tubes were now below the cylinders, oil fed to the rocker shafts was free to flow back into the sump.

Precisely to what degree Moore was involved in the development of this engine, if at all, it is difficult to say, but design drawings for the NSU engine clearly illustrate a three-bearing crankshaft with four crankpins. Whether Porsche ever designed a layout as bizarre as the one suggested by Moore is purely a matter for conjecture. Porsche had always looked for alternatives, not all of which were put into practice, and maybe Moore did see such a design at the bureau, but it seems unlikely that an engineer of Porsche's standing would have seriously considered anything like the design outlined by Moore.

The cooling arrangement for the engine was by the familiar sheet-metal cowl which was mounted above the engine and enclosed the power unit. A turbine fan was mounted on the end of the combined generator/starter shaft, circulating a strong current of air around the light-metal cylinder heads. A flexible hose was connected to the top of the fan cowling and run to a point near the right-hand rear wheel, presumably to help induce a steady current of cooling air. An integrated gearbox and differential unit was mounted to the fore of the axle, and the chassis was of the central box-type, similar to that fitted to the Zündapp, but now forked at the rear to form an engine cradle. Independent suspension was achieved by Porsche's new torsion-bar design. Torsion bars, of course, were nothing new, and had been used on British army vehicles as far back as 1906. A torsion bar is made up from a number of metal strips held firmly together, which, when held at one end whilst being twisted at the other, create a resistance which turns the bar into a form of spring. Although a fairly old idea in principle, the way in which Porsche used it was certainly new. He

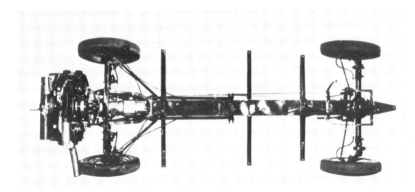

The NSU frame shown here is similar to that of the Zündapp but of 'U' profile and forked at the rear to form an engine cradle. The idea of using the frame like this seems to have originated from the Tatra company, although Karl Rabe, whilst working for Austro-Daimler after Porsche had left, had in fact modified one of Porsche's designs for the ADR series. He fitted the engine into a central-tube chassis forked at the front to form an engine cradle, with swing axles at the rear. This prompted unsuccessful legal action over patents by Tatra. A steel plate encloses the central 'U' frame. This was shaped like a piece of guttering to which the body was attached before outriggers were added for greater stability. Note the side-mounted torsion bars at the rear, and on this chassis a transverse leaf spring is also fitted, possibly to ease the stress on the rear torsion bars by the use of long trailing arms. A combined generator and starting motor is visible in a rather inaccessible position to the fore 'of the fan housing.

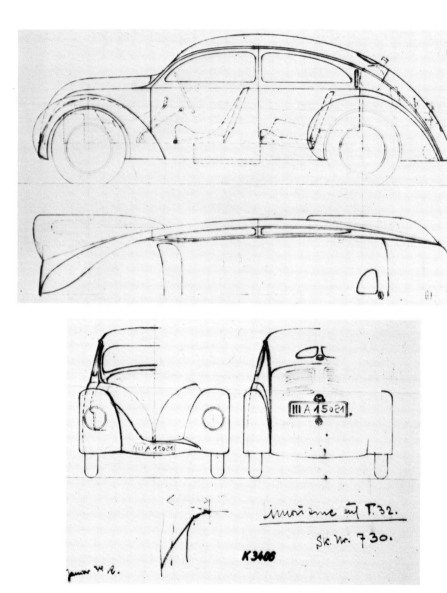

In this drawing of the Type 32 NSU that familiar profile begins to emerge. On the leather-bodied cars, as seen here, the headlamps are integrated into the wings.

36

splined the ends of the torsion bars to trailing arm-links carrying the steering stub axles at the front where, on the NSU design, there was a single cross-member tube mounted at the head of the frame. This housed both torsion bars which crossed one another, and were connected to the lower trailing links, the unsprung, top trailing links housed friction-type shock absorbers. At the rear, the long trailing arms of the type used on the Zündapp were now splined to torsion bars mounted longitudinally either side of the central member where they were held in brackets attached to the side-members. At the other end, they were hinged to the half-axle casings. Hydraulic shock-absorbers were also fitted at the rear. The use of these very long trailing arms at the rear was to create problems with the torsion bars, as became evident from an account in one of Porsche's torsion-bar patents taken out on 1 November 1935. This mentions the stresses imposed on the torsion bars due to the extra leverage created by the distance from the half-axle, which undoubtedly led to the torsion-bar failures experienced during trials. The report went on to outline the later method of housing the rear torsion bars in transverse tubes, as at the front, with much shorter trailing arms.

Porsche first registered patents on his new torsion-bar designs on 10 August 1931. This brings up a rather interesting little story which took place on 28 January 1932, when Porsche was awaiting the results on his new torsion-bar designs from Mickl, the mathematician. Josef Mickl had worked in the War Department designing aeroplanes with Porsche engines during the war, and now worked for Porsche as well as attending Stuttgart University where he had access to specialised equipment. Mickl had been commissioned by Porsche to carry out proving tests on the new bars. The final breakthrough came after days of watching and waiting with great anticipation on the part of Porsche and chief designer Rabe whilst Mickl completed his experiments, which involved placing the torsion bars under full stress. Suddenly, after a long and agonising wait, Mickl suddenly announced to an elated Porsche the good news that his torsion bars had passed the crucial test, and would work. Ghislaine Kaes recalls how he and Mickl were both running up a flight of steps, when Kaes turned and saw that Mickl was short of

Displaying strong resemblances to the Beetle, the all-steel bodied (*above*) NSU car has often been attributed mistakenly to Reutter but was in fact bodied by Drauz of Heilbronn, while the other two wood and leather bodied cars, of which one is shown here (*below*), were from Reutter.

breath. Kaes inquired sarcastically whether anything was wrong and Mickl replied, 'My qualities are not in my legs.'

The bodywork, by Erwin Komenda, was contracted out to two different coachbuilders. Two were built at the Reutter works at Stuttgart using the Weymann method of a wooden frame covered with leather, whilst the third, possibly with the production model in mind, was built by Drauz of Heilbronn, and was of all-steel construction.

In appearance the cars were fairly similar. The two Reutter cars had engine-cooling louvres situated at the rear and one had a slightly curved windshield. The Drauz car had engine louvres behind the rear side-windows like the Zündapps, and headlamps integrated into the tops of the wings. Body lines lay somewhere between its predecessors and the later Beetle. In profile it bore a strong resemblance to the latter, but the wheelbase was longer. Its overall length of 9.5ft (2,900mm), with a correspondingly wider body of about 4.9ft (1,500mm), high ground clearance created by the central frame, and the absence of a central tunnel, also made for a roomier interior. The frugal bodywork of the NSU design with minimum of overhang at front and rear, giving that wheels-in-the-corners look, was to set a pattern for the Volkswagen. The body was bolted to the central chassis-member to begin with, but this proved too narrow, and held the body too near to the centre line. It subsequently broke away, and outriggers were added to the frame to form a more stable mooring.

On 27 July 1934 the first road tests were undertaken. The 1470cc engine, developing 28bhp at 2600rpms, proved to be quite satisfactory, with a top speed of around 72mph (115kph). It was extremely noisy, which prompted Falkenhayn, obviously endowed with a dry sense of humour, to remark, after a ride in Porsche's latest offering, that it 'sounds like a worn-out stone-crusher'. Modifications did succeed in quietening it a little.

NSU then received a communication from Fiat reminding them about the agreement preventing them from re-entering the car-market. This put an end to Project 32, but neither party grieved over this situation as, by this time, Porsche had found himself another client—the new Chancellor, Adolf Hitler—and NSU were soon to be busy supplying motorcycles for the military. Falkenhayn, a fair-minded individual, allowed Porsche to retain the prototypes along with financial compensation. One of the three cars survived the war and, after spending many years in storage, was acquired by an NSU employee, who renovated it and placed the headlamps in the wings. It was later purchased by the Wolfsburg Works Museum, where it has remained ever since.

3

A Car for the Nation

Although obviously aware of the changes taking place in Germany, Porsche could not possibly have foreseen the strange chain of events which were to lead to the new Chancellor acting as sole benefactor to his small-car scheme, not only providing the funds for his new creation, but also building a factory to produce it.

The 1933 Berlin Motor Show, an annual event which was to be held that year on 11 February, was to take on a special significance, being used as the venue for Hitler's first major speech following his election as Chancellor. The speech came as a surprise to his industrial audience, for Hitler, apart from his dictatorial ambitions, was also, it seems, a keen motoring enthusiast displaying a considerable knowledge and understanding of the motor trade and its problems. He said, 'A nation is no longer judged by the length of its railway network but by the length of its highways.' He made promises about the creation of a new road network across the country and legislation aimed at easing the burdens of vehicle ownership by reducing taxes, relaxing stringent traffic laws, and making it considerably easier to acquire a driving licence; in fact, measures aimed at encouraging private ownership of cars and which would hopefully, help to raise the motoring industry out of its depression.

In spite of considerable reluctance from many of those present to take seriously Hitler's projections for a super highway network across Germany and a small car for the working masses, the industry as a whole seems to have been duped by Hitler's optimism and sympathetic overtures towards their current problems. Hitler, of course, was well aware of the political capital to be made out of emotive issues such as private car ownership, particularly at a time when the ordinary working man—the bulk of the electorate—walked to work, often after a long and hard day's toil. There were also the restrictions placed on families who had to rely on public transport for outings and holidays. To them a private car was nothing more than a dream. However, there were also somewhat more sinister motives behind Hitler's schemes for motorising the German people.

Hitler's small-car ideas appear to have evolved some years previously, possibly as early as 1923 whilst he was serving a sentence in Landsberg prison for riotous behaviour. Amongst his reading matter there was a biography of Henry Ford and Hitler came to be an admirer of him. It was, however, his friendship with the Mercedes car salesman, Jacob Werlin, which was to have one of the greatest influences on his future small-car ideas. The friendship was to become progressively closer with the passing of the years, and Werlin eventually became Hitler's chief adviser on motoring matters. In fact it was only two weeks before Hitler came to power that Werlin, possibly because of his affiliations with Hitler, was dismissed from his post with Mercedes, only to be reinstated the moment Hitler became Chancellor. Not only was he reinstated, but he was also promoted to the board of directors. The motivations for this sudden turnabout was the obvious usefulness of someone like Werlin as a means of gaining favour with the new Chancellor, and who better than Hitler to put up the money for a new racing team—something which Germany was in great need of at that time.

Porsche's first meeting with Hitler took place in April 1933 in connection with a racing project. In 1932 Porsche had decided it was time to design a new racing car. His keen interest in motor sport went back to before World War I with cars like the ones raced in the Prince Henry Trials, and later with the mighty Mercedes sports cars of the 'twenties. This had not been seen officially in racing events for almost four years, and Porsche became convinced that it was time somebody built a car capable of taking on the increasing foreign opposition.

After discussions with his finance director, Adolf Rosenberger, it was decided to establish a company called Hochleistungs to specialise in the development of high-performance engines. Their new racing car, called the 'P Wagen' after its creator, was designed with the recent Grand Prix weight regulations in mind, which limited cars to a maximum of 1,653.8lb (750kg). It resulted from the combined efforts of Josef Kales (who designed the engine), Karl Fröhlich (gearbox), Josef Zahradnik, (front and rear axle and steering) Erwin Komenda (bodywork) and Josef Mickl (mathematician).

Who was to manufacture this car when everyone in the business was struggling to make ends meet? It is doubtful whether any individual company would have given the idea a second thought, and this, it seems, is where the combined forces of the amalgamated companies of Horch, Audi, DKW and, more recently, Wanderer—known as Auto Union—came into the picture. Porsche had already clearly illustrated his abilities to both the Horch company of Zwickau in 1931 with a swing-axle design, and of course the Wanderer company, and Auto Union agreed to take on the project.

The car made its début in January 1934. It must have given the racing fraternity quite a nasty shock as it looked more like an aircraft fuselage on wheels than a racing car! The Auto Union P Rennwagen, which had been built at the Horch works, sported an ultra-lightweight body, constructed, along the lines of an aircraft, from light alloy with doped-fabric side panels specifically aimed at keeping weight to a minimum. The 16-cylinder V engine developing some 295bhp to start with was fitted at the rear directly behind the drivers' seat with a five-speed gearbox further on down in the tail. Porsche's system of independent trailing-arm suspension was fitted at the front with swinging half-axles at the rear suspended, on the prototype, by a central-leaf spring.

The success story of Porsche's Auto Union racing car has since become a legend. Even during its earliest trials the car set up a number of new records, and in 1934 won no less than three Grand Prix. In 1935 Hans Stuck, driving a streamlined version, broke the flying-mile record, achieving a speed of 199mph (320kph).

In its later development Porsche's wonder car, driven by Bernd Rosemeyer notched up a formidable number of victories, with speeds of up to 250mph (402kph), equal to racing cars even today, bringing much prestige to German motor racing.

43

However, in 1933 even Auto Union were reluctant to go it alone on what was, after all, a very expensive project, and felt it necessary to seek government financial assistance. As designer of the car, Porsche seemed to Auto Union the ideal person to put forward their case to Hitler, and so in the first week in April 1933, after a long journey across Germany to Berlin, Porsche came face to face with Hitler in the plush surroundings of the Kaiserhof Hotel. Porsche had in fact met Hitler once before back in 1926, through Werlin, at the motor races held outside Stuttgart. Porsche was already famous then, whereas Hitler was an almost unknown politician, and though Porsche had forgotten the meeting, Hitler had remembered it.

Hitler did not favour Auto Union as Germany's representative in the motor-racing field—no one had ever heard of them. He preferred Mercedes Benz, with their long established reputation and, besides, they had made a formal request for financial assistance a fortnight before. Nor did he see the necessity for having more than one racing team to represent the country.

Porsche's ability to explain technical matters in a way that was understood by the most non-technically minded individuals was to save the situation. He replied with a short lecture to which Hitler listened attentively. Porsche argued that no one German team could possibly take on the entire foreign opposition, and that what really mattered was the car and not the firm which produced it. He poured out details of the new design that would combine to give a power-to-weight ratio without equal. He said that the car would give the type of performance required to put Germany back amongst the world's leading competitors. As a result of this meeting Auto Union were promised at least some financial assistance for the project, and Hitler requested that he be kept regularly informed of future progress.

Ghislaine Kaes recalls that Hitler was impressed not only by what he had heard from Porsche about his new racing car, but also the way in which Porsche had put over Auto Union's case. It was this, together with the fact that they were both Austrian and could understand each other more readily, that helped to make him later Hitler's chosen designer of the people's car.

Various dates have been given for Porsche's first meeting with Hitler about the people's car, ranging from autumn 1933 to May 1934, by which time the small-car scheme was already well advanced. However, Hitler had been aware of Porsche's activities in this direction earlier, through their meetings about the Auto Union racing car. It is apparent from discussions with Ghislaine Kaes that the military, at Hitler's instigation, had shown a keen interest in Porsche's small car as a means of light transportation from the beginning. What Hitler did not gain from Porsche was relayed to him through Werlin (who was soon to be regarded as a nuisance by many in the motor industry).

It was during one of the meetings about the racing car that Hitler outlined his own ideas for a small car for the nation—which he referred to significantly as the 'Volkswagen'. Translated, of course, this means nothing more than 'people's car', and Hitler certainly did not intend that this term be adopted officially as a sort of trade name.

He stipulated a vehicle able to accommodate two adults and three children at a cruising speed of 60mph (100kph) over his new autobahns, returning a fuel consumption of 33mpg (6 litres per 100km). As the majority of owners would have limited finance, the cost of general maintenance and repairs would have to be kept to a minimum. As the car would spend most, if not all of its life out in the open, it was essential to have an air-cooled engine, as this would eliminate the hazards of frozen radiators and difficulties in starting during the winter. After all, the majority of its intended owners were off to work at the crack of dawn. So far Porsche was in agreement. But the crunch came when Hitler named the selling price, which was to be below 1,000 Reichsmark (the equivalent of a £100 car). At first he viewed this as impossible, for he himself had set the price in the region of 1,500 Reichsmark minimum.

Hitler then requested Porsche to forward details outlining his own ideas for the Volkswagen. This Porsche did in an exposé dated 17 January 1934, in which he wrote that a Volkswagen must not be a small car with reduced roadability, lasting but a short time only, with reduced overall measurements and increased weight. Instead a Volkswagen must be an everyday car, with common measurements and low weight, and all this achieved by entirely new ideas.

He then went on to outline the basic requirements for such a vehicle:

The best possible suspension and road-holding characteristics
A maximum speed of around 60mph (100kph)
Ability to climb a 30 per cent hill
A closed body for four persons
The lowest possible purchase price, as well as the lowest possible running costs.

He also added:

I understand by a people's car not a small car which, through the contrived reduction of its dimensions, of its performance, of its weight etc, carries on the old traditions. Such a car can be cheap to buy, but can never be cheap to use if only because its value to the consumer is very low owing to the reduction in comfort and durability.

In times of increasing traffic density, when driving safety merits increased attention, all measures aimed at reducing the consumer value of such a vehicle must be rejected out of hand. I therefore understand by a people's car only a genuine, practical, everyday vehicle which can challenge other everyday vehicles on equal terms. Thus, in the case of the future people's car, there must be no question of a compromise solution. In fact a new basic design solution must be sought which will enable the price to remain acceptable for a wide section of the population and will also be in step with technical progress for many years to come.

He also commented that the car he envisaged must maintain high resale value and be designed to assure a full measure of safety for the driver and passengers.

Hitler's speech at the 1934 Berlin Motor Show, which was held in March, clearly indicated that Porche's ideas for the Volkswagen had been studied for, after a brief opening speech, he said:

As long as the car is a vehicle for the rich, it is with bitter feelings on my part that millions of good, hard-working and industrious people will be excluded from the use of a motor vehicle, which would be particularly beneficial to the less well off, and which would not only prove useful to their way of life, but would also enhance their Sundays and holidays, giving them a great deal of future happiness. It is a problem which must be faced with courage, for what is not possible in one year may be possible in ten.

Once again Hitler had put forward promises of a cheap vehicle for the nation, and this set the ball rolling for Porsche. After a considerable amount of ministerial activity Hitler came up with a scheme to keep the price below the figure of 1,000 Reichsmark. He ordered the scheme to be put in the hands of the RDA (the Society of German Automobile Manufacturers), whose members would undertake (willingly or otherwise) to produce the components in their factories.

On 12 April Porsche received a communication from the Ministry of Transport (Reichverkehrsministerium or 'RVM') in Berlin containing a list of those who were to be put in charge of the Volkswagen operation. This included leading members of the RVM and personnel from the Department of Finance (the Reichskanzlerei), the Department of Industry (the Reichswirtschafts Ministerium). the Reichspropaganda Ministerium, and the RDA. The document also confirmed a selling price, further trimmed to keep the purchasing cost to a minimum, of 900 Reichsmark. The car would have to be capable of accommodating three adults and one child. A footnote of some significance and absolute proof of Hitler's military designs on the people's car stipulated the following: that the Volkswagen must be capable of carrying three soldiers and one machine gun plus ammunition. It seems almost certain that Porsche had to agree to the car's military application before being finally offered the contract to produce the civilian version.

On 12 May, from preliminary sketches, Hitler decided that the front hood should carry a lower profile to aid streamlining. Porsche then received a request from Herr Allmers to attend discussions at the offices of the RDA, before finally signing a lengthy contract dated 22 June 1934 for the motorisation of the German people's car. The contract stated the following: that the final cost of the car was to be 900 Reichsmark based on an output of 50,000 vehicles; Porsche was to be allocated a meagre budget of 200,000 Reichsmark (approximately £20,000) to cover the cost of designing and building three prototypes, and these had to be completed and handed over to the RDA for testing in ten months.

This was certainly a formidable undertaking and Porsche must have felt somewhat overwhelmed; but what were the alternatives? Turning down the offer might mean losing forever the opportunity to fulfil what

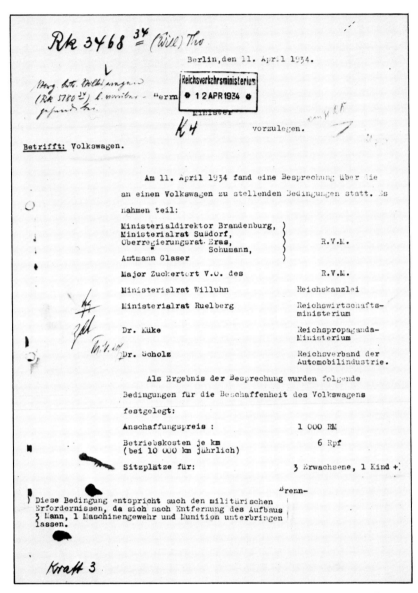

Rk 3468 ³⁴ = (Wille) Tho.

Berlin, den 11. April 1934.

May btr. Volkswagen?
(Rk 5780 ³⁴) l. vorüber - Herrn **Reichsverkehrsministerium** **● 1 2 APR 1934 ●**
gefunden. ~~Minister~~

K 4   vorzulegen.

Betrifft: Volkswagen.

Am 11. April 1934 fand eine Besprechung über die an einen Volkswagen zu stellenden Bedingungen statt. Es nahmen teil:

Ministerialdirektor Brandenburg,)
Ministerialrat Sußdorf,)
Oberregierungsrat Eras,) R.V.M.
        Schumann,)
Amtmann Glaser)

Major Zuckertort V.O. des   R.V.M.

Ministerialrat Willuhn   Reichskanzlei

Ministerialrat Ruelberg   Reichswirtschafts-
                                    ministerium

Dr. Küke   Reichspropaganda-
                                    Ministerium

Dr. Scholz   Reichsverband der
                                    Automobilindustrie.

Als Ergebnis der Besprechung wurden folgende Bedingungen für die Beschaffenheit des Volkswagens festgelegt:

Anschaffungspreis :   1 000 RM

Betriebskosten je km   6 Rpf
(bei 10 000 km jährlich)

Sitzplätze für: 3 Erwachsene, 1 Kind +.

                                          Brenn-
) Diese Bedingung entspricht auch den militärischen
Erfordernissen, da sich nach Entfernung des Aufbaus
3 Mann, 1 Maschinengewehr und Munition unterbringen
lassen.

Kraft 3

Firm proof of Hitler's military intentions for the Volkswagen: A German Ministry of Transport document signed by high dignitaries requiring that the car should have room for three men, a machine gun and ammunition, in addition to the earlier requirements that the selling price should be less than 1,000 Reichsmark and the seating should accommodate three adults and one child.

48

was probably his greatest ambition. His determination to press on regardless was made even more resolute by the unpleasant jibes from a member of the RDA who, after witnessing the signing and congratulating Porsche on his contract, suggested that he had taken on an impossible assignment. The brief time allowed under the contract ruled out any totally new design, leaving little alternative but to use the NSU Type 32 as a basis for further development. He may in fact have already had this in mind when he forwarded his exposé on 17 January.

Although Porsche did not get the final go-ahead until June, the first sketch, number 804, had been completed on 27 April and survives today in the Porsche museum. By June sufficient progress had been made to derive the first weight statistics—a very crucial factor—for two initial prototypes, of 1,201.5lb (544.9kg) and 1,084.9lb (492kg), the second car being an open tourer.

Before any real progress could be made, however, a number of critical problems had to be overcome. Firstly, in order to keep costs to a minimum, the power unit, which was to be fitted at the rear (and just about the most expensive part of any motor car), whilst capable of matching the laid-down requirements, would have to be of a type that would be cheap to manufacture. To this end, a 2-stroke seemed to fit the bill, as this eliminated the costly valve gear of the 4-stroke engine. But 2-strokes suffer a number of marked disadvantages, in particular shorter engine life. They also lack the braking abilities of a 4-stroke when the throttle is closed, and this in turn would mean larger and more expensive brakes.

In order to achieve a satisfactory power-to-weight ratio the body would have to be as light as possible, whilst remaining sufficiently robust to withstand a considerable degree of punishment. Bearing in mind that this car was to be driven at a sustained speed of 60mph (100kph) on as little petrol as possible, it needed a body of advanced aerodynamic shape. The art of streamlining of course was nothing new to Porsche and, in order to save time and money, the previous design for NSU was used as a basis for further development.

The Volkswagen project was called Type 60. The office was now becoming a hive of activity as Porsche's team grappled with the prob-

49

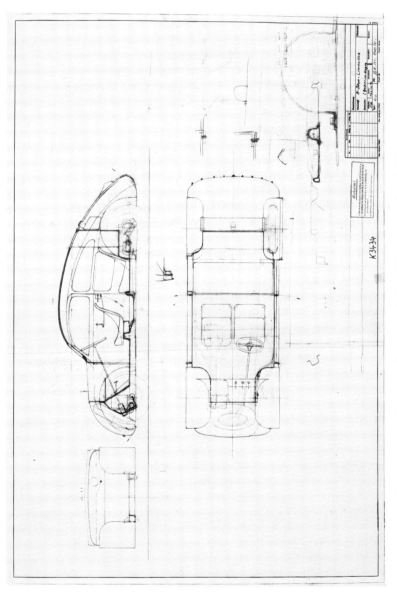

K34·34

The very first Type 60 drawing of the Volkswagen, dated 27 April 1934. Amongst later refinements to this early profile, evolved from NSU blueprints, was the lowering of the front hood, on Hitler's instructions, to aid streamlining and give the drop-away bonnet we know today.

lems of designing Hitler's car for the nation (or was it the army ?). Drawings appeared in quick succession in the quest for the perfect combination of functional but attractive body styling with an engine that was cheap to run but sufficiently powerful, and all this within the strict cost limitations.

To save money, Porsche installed a workshop in the garage of his house in Stuttgart, with a staff of fifty to begin work on the testing of engines and the assembly of the first prototypes.

When Hitler addressed the 1935 Berlin Motor Show in February, he was surprisingly optimistic, in view of the fact that it was to be a further six months before the completion of the first prototypes. He said:

> I am happy to announce that, through the abilities of the brilliant engineer, Porsche, and his staff, it has been possible to complete preliminary plans of the German Volkswagen, and examples will be tested in the middle of this year. It must be possible to present the German people with a car that is no dearer than a medium-price motorcycle and, like a motorcycle, be also moderate on petrol.

This final statement brings to light an interesting conversation that Ghislaine Kaes had with Hitler's driver shortly after the war, in which the latter recalls that whilst travelling with Hitler on the way to one of his political venues in pouring rain, Hitler noticed a rather bedraggled pair of motorcyclists just up ahead, and turned to his driver and said that it should be possible to produce a car costing no more than a medium-priced motorcycle.

Porsche's designers experimented with a variety of engines during late 1934, and early 1935. Certainly the most interesting of these was the 'A' motor, a vertical twin cylinder two-stroke, each cylinder with two bores, one of the pistons acting as a pump piston. This favourite of Porsche's was of the same design as that used on the Austrian Puch motorcycle and, according to progress reports which were handed into the RDA, was built in at least two different sizes—that of 850cc, and the A1 of 1,000cc. Alas, this particular power unit was doomed to failure through overheating of the pistons. Probably the most bizarre were the 'C' motor, a single-sleeve valve design which, judging from line drawings, was probably around 850cc, and yet another which, despite

51

modifications from its designer, Kales, consistently broke sleeve connecting rods. Then there was 'D' motor by Engelbrecht, a 2-cylinder boxermotor which, again judging from line drawings, was probably around 850cc. Although a great deal simpler than the other two, this one proved totally inadequate and insufficiently flexible, particularly in the lower gears. A 3-cylinder radial also came up for consideration, but does not appear to have got beyond the drawing-board stage. However, the problem of finding a suitable power unit was still no nearer to being solved. It was designer Reimspiess who, after rejoining Porsche in September 1934, came up with the answer.

Franz Xaver Reimspiess, another Austrian, had joined Austro Daimler at the age of seventeen as an errand boy. One day out of curiosity he had entered the drawing office, been fascinated by what he had seen and managed to persuade his superiors to let him try his hand. It seems that he never looked back.

It was late in 1934, whilst Reimspiess was working on the Auto Union project concerning modifications for the front brakes, which were being enlarged to cope with increased power output, and also the rear suspension, which was now to be by torsion bars instead of leaf spring, that, whilst passing Porsche in the drawing office, Reimspiess noticed drawings for a small vw 400cc engine, further details unknown, and remarked on the inefficiency of the design. Porsche asked him if he thought that the new rear torsion-bar design was too weak, to which Reimspiess replied that no component is ever too strong. Reimspiess then put forward his own ideas for a 4-cylinder, horizontally opposed engine, of the type fitted to the NSU. After some persuasion, Porsche, who was now impressed more than ever before with this old Austro Daimler designer, gave him the go-ahead. It took Reimspiess just forty-eight hours to produce the blueprints for the Volkswagen engine virtually as we know it today which, in modified form, went on to power over eighteen million Beetles around the world. But Reimspiess came under strong opposition from the other members of the team who felt that a 4-cylinder unit would prove far too dear and teased him with 'How goes it with your Rolls Royce engine?' That is, until Herr Kux, another bureau mathematician, announced that Reimspiess's cylinders

IIIA-34993

The bodywork of the V1 (*above*) and the V2 (*over*) was of wood and metal, distinguishable by the rounded front boot lid with a central opening knob. At the rear both cars had broad louvring stretching the entire width of the engine lid with identical rib-moulding contours. The rear intake, in common with all the prototypes, acted as a sort of venetian blind, permitting partial rear vision. A glass partition in the saloons separated the engine compartment from the passenger's compartment.

These pictures depict the cars in 1937 when, acting as staff cars for Porsche and his team, bumpers were added and the headlamps, formerly recessed into the front hood, were moved into the wings.

actually worked out $13\frac{1}{2}$ Reichsmark cheaper than any of the 2-cylinder units then under development. Porsche awarded Reimspiess 100 Reichsmark for this engine, which was to show its superiority during the forthcoming road tests.

By summer of 1935, the first prototypes were nearing completion and by early December, a saloon called the V1, and a cabriolet, the V2, were to be seen trundling through the Black Forest. Even at this early stage they had the distinctive outline of the all-familiar Beetle. The V1 coachwork was attributed to Reutter and the V2 to Drauz.

The V1

The V2

Conceived from the earlier NSU prototypes, this first of the line of central-tube backbone platform frames, but without the wooden floor, was the type used on the V1 and V2. This one is fitted with the inflexible 2-cylinder boxermotor, the last unit to be tried before Reimspiess' engine. Note the two carburettors.

From the backbone frame of the earlier prototypes came the first vw platform frame. Although similar in many ways to that which we know today, the ones fitted to the V1 and V2 were part metal and part wood, with a pressed-steel, central, tubular backbone with outriggers, forked at the rear to form an engine cradle and wooden floor pan, made up from plywood sections inserted in the frame. The now world-famous, torsion-bar suspension system was in place with twin tubular cross-members mounted at the head of the frame, carrying the Porsche worm-and-nut steering box and housing the upper and lower torsion bars fixed at the centre and splined at either end to parallel swinging levers carrying the steering-stub axles. At the rear, a single transverse member housed the rear torsion bars splined to

spring plates attached to the half-axle casings. As a cost saving, brakes were mechanical.

Another Berlin Motor Show was to take place before the three pilot cars were ready to be handed over to the RDA and once again Hitler gave his own annual speech to the motor manufacturers. As optimistic as ever, he announced:

> I don't doubt that the genius of the designers and later the producers of the car will make it possible to produce a car that is within the financial means of the broad masses of our people, as has been done in America—a shining example to us.

What he did not point out, was that the average German would at that time have to work approximately three times as many hours as his American counterpart to purchase and maintain a low-priced vehicle and probably even more so, as petrol in the USA was a good deal cheaper than in Europe.

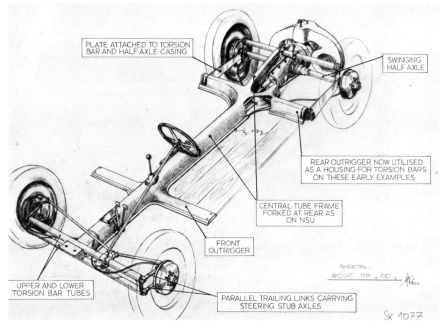

PLATE ATTACHED TO TORSION
BAR AND HALF AXLE CASING

SWINGING
HALF AXLE

REAR OUTRIGGER NOW UTILISED
AS A HOUSING FOR TORSION BARS
ON THESE EARLY EXAMPLES

CENTRAL TUBE FRAME
FORKED AT REAR AS
ON NSU

FRONT
OUTRIGGER

UPPER AND LOWER
TORSION BAR TUBES

PARALLEL TRAILING LINKS CARRYING
STEERING STUB AXLES

The first Volkswagen central-tube platform frame, with the Doppelkolben motor. This drawing from 1935 clearly illustrates the way in which a central-tube backbone frame first evolved into a platform frame with the floor and central frame member integrated, as fitted to the V1 and V2. The floor was made of wood and the top transverse member at the rear appears to have functioned as a stop to limit vertical movement of the half-axles.

Herr Almers and the other members of the RDA were now convinced more than ever before that the whole idea would amount to nothing and that Hitler's optimistic speeches were little more than political gimmickry. But they had reckoned without Porsche's hell-bent determination to see things through at any price, and on 5 February 1936 the first of the three pilot cars, designated vw3 (signifying the number built) was completed and ready for preliminary testing. The bodies of the vw3s were built in a special department at the Daimler-Benz factory in Stuttgart, manned by Porsche's own staff. Cars 1 and 2 had bodies constructed using a wooden frame fabricated with sheet metal, whereas car 3 had an all-steel body. After being involved in an accident, car 2

58

The three cars of the vw3 series were almost identical. Their overall length was 3.9m (12.8ft), and width and height were both 1.5m (4.9ft). In common with the V1 and V2 headlamps were fitted into recesses in the front hood, but the front boot lid was now straight with opening knobs on either side.

had to be rebuilt utilising the remaining serviceable components from the crashed car. Consequently, it did not re-join the others until just before the official trials, by which time, car 3 had covered some considerable distance including entry in the 1936 Alpine trials, the Alps also being used to test the cars in extremes of climate and on steep gradients.

Similar in appearance to the V1, the cars were all powered by Reimspiess's 4-cylinder, overhead-valve boxermotor, with a displacement of 984cc, a compression ratio of 5.8:1 and developing 22bhp at 3,000-3,200rpms, with a top speed of 64.4mph (103.6kph). The engine was situated aft of the rear axle, with an integrated gearbox and differential to the fore of the axle giving suitably balanced weight distribution. The now fully evolved platform frame was an all-steel construction, with an

Two rear views of the vw3 series, showing the rounded air intake peculiar to it. The second car shown differs slightly from the other two in the series in rear deck contouring. At least one of the cars later had its headlamps moved into the wings in the fashion of the vw30s.

integrated central-tube backbone frame and floor pan. To keep the selling price down to 900 Reichsmark a radically new approach to production techniques would be required. Porsche was prompted to study first-hand the American mass-production techniques which had made possible the American motoring success. He spent several weeks touring the vast American industry, noting in great detail not only the latest machinery in operation but also pay structures and working conditions. He stopped off in Britain on his return, where he visited the Austin works at Longbridge but, compared with the United States, the

Porsche's favourite, the Doppelkolben motor, a twin-cylinder air-cooled design with each cylinder divided into two bores. One piston is on the inlet side and the other on the exhaust side, acting as a pump piston for the expulsion of exhaust gases. The main advantage of this arrangement was the more efficient segregation of induction vapour and exhaust gases, thus more efficient detonation. The flaw was the overheating of the exhaust pistons by the exhaust gases, and the side-mounted fan proved a poor substitute for external air currents. Each pair of pistons shared a common crankpin. The large object on the right is a combined generator and starting motor. The inset shows the fully assembled engine.

The inflexible 2-cylinder boxermotor discarded in favour of Reimspiess' 4-cylinder unit.

British motoring industry was rather a primitive affair, and Porsche headed for home, arriving back in Stuttgart on 14 November. Naturally Hitler was interested in Porsche's findings and these were quickly relayed to him.

On 12 October 1936, some eighteen months after the original deadline had expired, the three prototypes were handed over to the RDA for road-testing and general assessment. This required each car to cover a minimum distance of 30,000 miles (50,000km). To accomplish this, each car would be driven virtually day and night over two carefully selected routes. The first, using a long stretch of autobahn, would take the cars from Stuttgart to Bad Nauheim via Karlsruhe and Frankfurt—approximately 300 miles (480km). The second, through mountainous terrain, ran from Stuttgart via Pforzheim, Baden Baden, Offenburg, Kniebis and Freudenstatt, taking in parts of the Black Forest.

Porsche's garage acted as operations centre, with the cars coming in, being refuelled and then heading out once more on the alternative route.

The complex Schiebermotor, a single-sleeve valve design. The sleeve cam and gear can be clearly seen in the left-hand crank web. The advantage of this design was the reduction in servicing costs by eliminating the periodic adjustment required with tappet valves. The sleeves, which fitted within the bore, had induction and exhaust ports coinciding with those of the cylinder. Each sleeve had its own conrod which was actuated by the single cam mounted centrally and driven by a gear from the crankshaft. This in turn caused the sleeve to rotate within the cylinder until the ports of both the sleeve and cylinder were aligned to an open position at the appropriate points in the cycle. A torsion-bar spring returned the sleeve, thus closing the ports. One of the sleeves with the ports uppermost can be seen in the foreground. Broken con-rods and a high rate of friction ruled out this engine as a viable contender and it reputedly never got beyond bench testing.

The 3.8 Wanderer acted as recovery vehicle for breakdowns which occurred during the course of these punishing trials. Each RDA examiner made a detailed account of the car's performance, with even the smallest faults and occurrences being meticulously recorded. A massive dossier of facts, figures and incidents was built up, ranging from brake failures to burnt-out valves and broken con-rods. One car collided with a deer whilst roaring down the autobahn, but was able to return, with the unfortunate animal in the back (which was later to provide a tasty feast).

The tests were completed just a few days before Christmas, and the formidable volume of records was handed over to Herr Vorwig, technical officer of the RDA, who then compiled a detailed analysis and assessment for the Ministry of Transport. The road tests had revealed a number of weaknesses, as might be expected of any new vehicle subjected to such an ordeal. One major problem which plagued all three was broken crankshafts, which were cast rather than forged. The problem was solved by fitting the latter type, a practice adhered to by VW ever since. In Herr Vorwig's summing up, he stated the following:

> The design has up to now proved serviceable. In general the cars did well in the 30,000 mile test. A number of weak points and defects were discovered; however, these were not of a fundamental nature and can probably be rectified without great difficulty from a technical point of view. One or two assemblies, such as front axles and the brakes, still require thorough testing so that they can be developed further. The consumption of fuel has been kept within satisfactory limits.
>
> The performance and handling characteristics of the car are good. Thus the vehicle has shown good characteristics which make further development appear desirable.

Herr Vorwig's summing up was fair to a degree, and his seeming lack of enthusiasm merely reflected the antipathy of the other members of the RDA. As Herr Vorwig was reported to have said some years later it was obvious at the time that a privately owned motor industry had no interest in a people's car which would compete against their own products. Certainly Hitler's decision to entrust the task of producing the Volkswagen to Porsche may well have sparked off a certain amount

Reimspiess' 4-cylinder boxermotor seen here in 1937, with the addition of the oil cooler similar to that fitted to its modern counterpart. Indeed, the engine differed surprisingly little from that known to millions of Beetle owners throughout the world. The cylinders, with separate detachable heads, are in two banks, with each pair lying horizontally on either side of the crankshaft. Each pair of opposed pistons, which are slightly staggered, drives the crankshaft. This has three main bearings with four separate crankpins. The design employs overhead pushrod valves. The inclined pushrod tubes, which featured so prominently in the NSU–Walter Moore story, can be seen below the cylinder heads and, like the NSU, the camshaft lies below the crankshaft, from which it is driven by gears. The cooling system layout remains the same even today, and consists of a fan-belt pulley, mounted on the end of the crankshaft which, in turn, drives the pedestal-mounted generator with a turbine fan fixed to the end of the generator shaft. The fan and light-alloy cylinder heads are enclosed by a sheet-metal cowl. When the engine is in motion the fan circulates a current of air around the heavily finned cylinder heads. The cooling works in the same manner as a motorcycle—which is virtually what a vw engine is, except for the artificially-produced air current, provided by more natural means on a motorcycle when it is in motion. This method proved somewhat inadequate on the prototypes. Although the engine was designed to perform at comparatively low 'revs' to avoid over-exertion and thus achieve a longer engine life (in fact, one of the main reasons for its renowned longevity), it was still prone to overheating, which led to the hideous louvring of the prototypes. The addition of an oil cooler in 1937, plus further modifications to the fan, reducing the reliance on external air currents, enabled the introduction of a rear window on the vw38 series.

Like much of the Volkswagen, the horizontally opposed engine had already been well tried. As early as 1898 Karl Benz had built such a design. In 1924 BMW were powering a motorcycle with a twin-cylinder boxermotor mounted transversely in the frame. Porsche is reputed to have taken a hand in this whilst working for Daimler Motoren. It was finally produced by a certain Herr Fritz who moved from the latter company to BMW, and the design can still be seen today. In 1928 Hans Ledwinka introduced his 4-cylinder 1.5-litre version and even when Porsche and his team were still developing the prototype Martin Stolle developed a superb specimen for the ill-fated 'NAG' and Jowet in England used a horizontal layout in their small lightweight cars. But it was Reimspiess' engine which was ultimately to become the most renowned of its type.

---

of professional jealousy amongst other members of the industry, who certainly did not go out of their way to assist Porsche.

In a meeting between Porsche and the RDA, following completion of the tests, questions were asked as to why, after the contract stipulated a completion period of ten months, the cars were not in fact handed over until eighteen months beyond the original date specified? Porsche replied with details of the problems of finding an engine sufficiently powerful and cheap to manufacture. He said that a number were developed and tested but had been found wanting. None performed so successfully as the 'flat four'. Problems were also encountered with the body structure. This had to be robust and so aluminium could not be used, with steel sheeting the only suitable alternative.

The reports were forwarded to the Ministry of Transport, with a suggestion from Herr Allmers that each manufacturer should compete by putting forward designs for its own people's car, an idea which was met with a sharp rebuff from the Chancellor.

The 1937 Berlin Motor Show, held on 20 February, led to another of Hitler's motoring speeches, despite the fact that he still had only a few rather basic prototypes to back up his latest claims.

It is now only necessary to make final arrangements before putting the Volkswagen into production. I would like to stress that it is a big mistake to believe that the production of a small car will reduce the sales potential of bigger vehicles, because people will not give up purchasing expensive cars because they wish to buy a cheaper one, but purely because they wish to buy a cheaper vehicle in the first place. This is why Germany will produce only one Volkswagen!

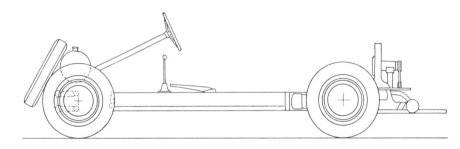

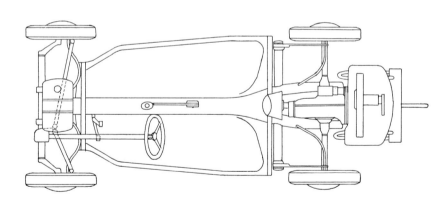

The fully evolved platform frame, from a drawing made in 1939. This example differs only slightly from that fitted to the vw3s of 1936, when the rear torsion bars housed in the outrigger and now a more integrated part of the frame was placed in a separate transverse tube.

A rear view of the vw3, showing the original 944cc vw boxermotor—almost a scaled-down version of its predecessor fitted to the nsu.

Herr Allmers and the members of the RDA had probably by now come to the conclusion that the whole idea was to be written off, particularly in view of the long delay in producing even the initial prototypes. Instead, as was quite evident from Hitler's speech, they were now to be faced with a vehicle that might put the whole lot of them out of business. If Hitler was not bluffing over the construction of Germany's new autobahns, and there was sufficient new tarmac being laid to know that he was not, then they had better take him seriously.

Hitler then issued the warning that either the car industry faced up to the problem of a vehicle for the nation or it would cease to be private (a hint at nationalisation).

Whilst touring the exhibits, Hitler was invited by Herr Opel to view his latest creation, the Opel P4, a small car obviously designed to compete with the Volkswagen, at a price of 1,450 Reichsmark. '. . . And this, my Fuhrer, is our Volkswagen', exclaimed Herr Opel, but before he could continue Hitler turned round and walked away. Any future plans Herr Opel may have had for his cheap vehicle were dashed when shortly afterwards the authorities took control of the supply of iron and steel, preventing Opel from obtaining the required allocation to build their small car.

Hitler then announced plans to set up a new company for the production of the Volkswagen. This was known as 'Gezuvor'. It was established on 18 May 1937, with its headquarters above the drawing offices of the Porsche office at 24 Kronenstrasse, under the management of Herr Direktor Otto Dyckhoff, a production and design expert. The new company, with an initial capital of almost half a million Reichsmark (£50,000) which was to come most conveniently from the

The fully evolved all-metal platform frame of the vw3 series, against a make-shift backcloth outside Porsche's garage at 48–50 Feurbacherweg. The fuel tank, absent in this photograph, was fitted at the front. Front and rear shock-absorbers, absent on the two earlier cars, are now in place. The spare wheel is housed in the front, as on the later Beetle, and even then this was seen as a useful safety feature. The battery well is clearly visible beneath the rear seat, in the later tradition.

'The people's car must be capable of carrying three soldiers, a machine gun and ammunition.' This military derivative first appeared in 1937, being little more than a crudely fabricated chassis from a redundant prototype.

coffers of the Deutsche Arbeitsfront of DAF (the Nazi German Trade Union). The Gezuvor was to be run jointly by Ferdinand Porsche, Bodo Lafferentz—the understudy of Dr Ley (chief of the DAF), whose main job was the building of the factory—and, needless to say, Werlin.

One of the first tasks for the new company ordered by Hitler was to make plans for the factory. But before any form of production could begin it would be necessary to continue development of the car. This led to the construction of a further batch of prototypes, this time no less than thirty, called Type 60 vw30 (a figure representing the number of cars to be produced). These were built at the Daimler-Benz factory in Stuttgart, not, it seems, with the blessing of the company, as they were helping to create what was now clearly a formidable competitor to their own vehicles.

71

Daimler-Benz had themselves experimented with a small rear-engined car in 1934—the '130'—powered by a 4-cylinder, in-line unit, with a displacement of 1,308cc, producing 26bhp at 3,200rpms. It featured a central-tube frame, forked at the rear, with swing-axle suspension. Capable of a top speed of 60mph (100kph), it did not, however, meet with a great deal of success because, unlike the vw, the weight distribution on this design caused the vehicle to be unstable.

Werlin, being Hitler's chief motoring adviser as well as a director of Daimler-Benz, was becoming an unwanted influence on the company, but they had to cooperate, as Hitler had made quite clear in his speech. It is quite conceivable that, had the other members of the motoring industry shown a little more foresight, they may well have shared in the fortunes of the people's car, but instead they resented bitterly the new state-financed Volkswagen company.

A vw30 chassis in the company of the V2, with a bodied vw30 in the back-ground. Otherwise the chassis is almost the same as in the VW3 model. Another notable feature of this series was the canister-type carburettor air cleaner, peculiar to these thirty prototypes.

It took just four months for the Porsche staff at Daimler-Benz to build the new series, which was finished to the traditionally high standard of the company. The cars were to undergo a long and punishing ordeal, covering a staggering $1\frac{1}{4}$ million miles (2 million kilometres), approximately 50,000 miles (100,000km) apiece, over the same route as the three former prototypes. The drivers for this marathon were provided by ss stormtroopers who were to man the cars around the clock. The ss, being sworn to secrecy as part of their work, were ideal for the job as they were to remain silent to a curious public. The cars were based at Kornwestheim army barracks outside Stuttgart, which possessed the necessary workshop facilities and fuel depot. The testing was quite a sophisticated business as the cars were fitted with a mass of instrumentation designed to record in detail almost every function, including the number of times the brakes, clutch and gear lever were operated. Certainly this was the first time in Europe that such a large number of prototypes had been subjected to this kind of detailed and rigorous testing.

Mechanically the cars were identical to the vw3s, but the design as a whole had been subject to further refinement based on the findings from the earlier testing. The vw30 engine possessed an oil cooler similar to its modern counterpart, which went part way to solving the high-temperature problems, but it still required a large air intake with heavy louvring continuing to take precedence over a rear window.

Obtaining ordinary machine hands for the factory would present little problem, but there was a desperate shortage of skilled engineers. Since the Depression after World War I many of these skilled workers had emigrated to the United States in search of better prospects and, in order to fill the gap, it was decided that Porsche, along with his secretary, Ghislaine Kaes, Werlin, Lafferentz and Dyckhoff should pay a visit to this country in search of old German citizens willing to return to the homeland to help man the new factory. The task of interviewing potential applicants was left to Werlin, Lafferentz and Dyckhoff, who offered bait in the form of high pay, free housing, educational facilities for their children, free insurance and even free removals back to Germany.

A vw30 (*left*) in the company of the V1. Note the reversion to a circular front luggage lid, similar to that of the V1 and V2 The doors are more heavily canted, at the cost of the rear passengers' windows. They opened from the front, as on all the prototypes, but this was later changed to prevent the doors flying open while the car was in motion—a tip Porsche had picked up whilst in the USA. On the Type 30 the door handles were also recessed.

Porsche in the meantime toured the industry to glean information on suitable machinery which, it was hoped, could be built in Germany. The timing could not have been more fortunate, as a team of Auto Union cars had been entered in the 1937 Vanderbilt trophy at Long Island on 5 July, and Porsche was able to watch Bernd Rosemeyer reach first place for the company in a spectacular event.

Porsche also achieved another long-awaited ambition when he met Henry Ford. They had an enthusiastic discussion through their interpreters, during which Porsche discussed details of his people's car. He asked Ford if he was worried by the prospect of someone else producing a competitor to his own small cheap cars, to which Ford replied that if someone else could build a more competitive vehicle than he could, then it served him right!

Lafferentz and company had managed to find a small group of engineers and their families willing to return to the fatherland (some of whom apparently went back to the States again at the outbreak of war).

The same cars viewed from the rear, showing the bee-hive louvring of the vw30 (*foreground*) and its familiar rear contours. (On the 1937 cars the central moulding continued on to the roof section where it broadened out to a plateau ending either side of the top of the front windshield.) Komenda had commenced this body design as long ago as 18 January 1936 under type 61K. This and the other prototypes tended to have an unnecessarily spartan appearance due to the absence of bumpers and general trim. Dimensions were the same as those of the vw3 series.

The thirty prototypes passed the rigorous testing with flying colours and from this series came the vw38 (marking the year of introduction) and the final stage of evolution for the Volkswagen with specifications which would remain almost entirely unaltered until well after the war. The engine capacity had been increased by 1cc to 985cc, increasing top speed to 65mph (105kph), but otherwise the car was mechanically identical to the vw30. It is possible but unconfirmed that the vw38s, also numbering thirty cars, were merely rebodied vw30 chassis, the bodywork this time attributable to Reutter & Co of Stuttgart. The most notable difference on these pre-production 'Versuchswagens', was the presence of the famous 'spectacles' rear window. This was possible because of the boosted output of the engine-cooling fan, which reduced the reliance on external air currents whilst the car was in motion.

The now fully evolved Volkswagen gave Hitler the opportunity to display his long-awaited people's car to a curious German public. The

Built entirely of wood, this mock-up of the vw38 was, in all probability, built by Reutter, who were responsible for the bodywork of the series. The clue to the composition of this design study are the wooden struts inside the car. Headlamps have still to be fully integrated into the wings. The absence of rear bumpers may have been due to the troubles of authenticity when working in wood, or may have been a cost-saving measure, on a car to cost less than 1,000 marks. The famous spectacles rear window, made possible by cooling modifications, can also be seen.

cars were sent across the length and breadth of Germany to add credibility to Hitler's promises to the nation.

In June 1938, Porsche switched the Volkswagen operation from 24 Kronenstrasse, which continued to function for other work, to the new planning offices for the Deutschen Volkswagen at 2 Spitalwaldstrasse, Stuttgart. This also became the new headquarters for the Gezuvor, which became the Volkswagenwerk GmbH on 6 September of that year, with the new planning offices going under the name of Dr Ing. hc F. Porsche KG.

The plans for the Volkswagen factory were completed on 4 January 1938, the most ambitious undertaking of its kind anywhere in the world. A main assembly building was to stretch for almost a mile covering a total ground area of 4 million sq ft (nearly 400,000sq m). Initially it was planned to employ two shifts of 10,000 and 7,000 men, progressing later to a workforce of 30,000. This would require an entirely new factory city to house the workers and their families, which, when completed, would accommodate a population of 90,000. The construction work began on the first properties in September 1938, under the auspices of a non-profit-making construction company. As it worked out, only about 10 per cent of the town was completed by the outbreak of war, with a total of 2,358 properties being built. Initial output of the factory was to be in the region of half a million cars per annum rising eventually to one and a half million.

Apart from its intended purpose, the new car plant, which was to cost 50 million Reichsmark—from the treasury of the DAF—was to serve as a prestigious industrial showpiece for the Third Reich. The creation of this masterpiece was entrusted to Peter Koller, a former student of Albert Speer, the wartime armaments minister and former architect.

A preview of the factory was arranged in a model display at the 1938 Berlin Motor Show as a promotional gimmick both for the German public and also for foreign customers, as it was Hitler's intention to sell the Volkswagen around the world. One of the two lavishly illustrated brochures came in English, French and Italian and car Type 66 was a right-hand drive model. Hitler's opening speech, needless to say, was centred around the Volkswagen:

> It took four years of continuous development to produce this model of the people's car. In our opinion we have produced a medium-priced car, and also a car that is easy to assemble, with the minimum workforce. This car, which was evolved out of Dr Porsche's years and years of work, will this year continue trial tests. This car will find millions of new buyers of the lower-income group to become car owners. There is no doubt we are indebted to our directors, engineers, foremen, workers and salesmen for the best car in the world. Today I am also convinced we will produce the cheapest car in the world.

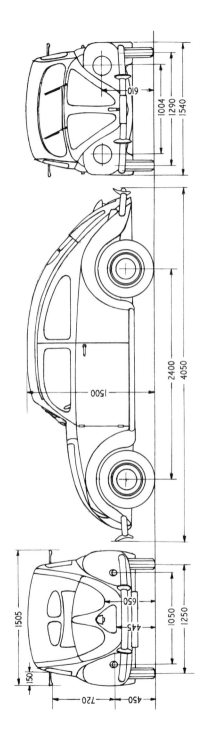

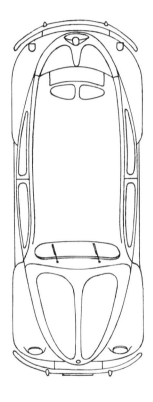

The blueprints for the KDF Karosseriewerk, showing the profile which in post-war years was to become a symbol of good engineering and reliability. It was simple and yet aerodynamically years ahead of most other competitors both before and after the war, and a shape which was to stand the test of time like no other vehicle in the history of the motor car.

The task of selecting a suitable location for the factory and town was given to Bodo Lafferentz, acting under orders from Robert Ley. To help him in his search, he hired an aircraft to carry out a mass aerial survey of potential sites. They required an area of flat terrain of about 20sq miles (50sq km). The final choice lay on the Mittelandkanal in lower Saxony, between Berlin and Hanover and a few miles from the town of Fallersleben. This site was ideally suited for an industrial installation as the canal linked the western industrial centres with the coalfields of the Ruhr and it was within easy link-up distance with the main railway line and could be made easily accessible by road. The majority of the land required belonged to the estate of Count Schulenburg, whose ancestral home was Wolfsburg castle. Lafferentz had full authority to make a compulsory purchase of all the land that was necessary, and the Count was required to forfeit two-thirds of his estate, along with some of his neighbours' property. The Count put up a brave fight but, despite friends in high places and every conceivable excuse he could levy at the authorities, including the preservation of oak trees and the infestation of insects, he eventually had to concede to the demands of the dictator.

On 26 May 1938, amidst swastica banners, Nazi brass hats and Hitler youth, Hitler laid the foundation stone of the new factory, with a speech in which he revealed the name of the new people's car.

> This car was produced for the broad masses, for their personal form of transport, to give them joy and happiness. This car can only have one name, and I shall give that name today. The car shall carry the name of the organisation who tried so hard to bring to the broad masses of our people joy and power. It shall be named KDF car—'*Kraft Durch Freude*' [meaning 'Strength Through Joy', after the strength-through-joy movement of the Deutschen Arbeitsfront—the DAF]. The factory shall be built out of the power of the whole German nation.

On hearing this fanciful name for his creation Porsche wondered how they were to sell a car bearing such a hideous name to the rest of the world. The president of the regional administration in Hanover decreed amalgamation of the communities of Rotherfelde, Rothehof, Hesslingen and parts of Sandkamp, Fallersleben and Hattorf to form a new community to be known under Hitler's decree as the '*Stadt des* KDF *Wagens*' (Town of the Strength-Through-Joy Cars).

The construction of the factory was put under way without delay, but the DAF labour force soon diminished as Hitler switched priorities to the western defences. The problem was solved, however, when Hitler called upon fellow dictator Mussolini to provide a fairly sizeable Italian labour force to complete the task on the main building, which from start to finish took little over eighteen months to complete.

By the time Hitler was ready to make his speech at the ceremony for laying the factory cornerstones, the price of the Volkswagen had risen to 990 Reichsmark. This was still relatively cheap, but as the average pay in Germany at that time was only 200-300 Reichsmark per month, there were not likely to be many cash customers queueing up to buy their first four-wheeled transport. The job of marketing was given to Robert Ley, who devised a rather ingenious savings scheme, which came into effect on 1 January 1939. Parodoxically it prevented anyone wealthy enough from purchasing a car outright. Details of the savings plan were outlined in one of the KDF brochures.

The possibility of owning a people's car was open to every German citizen, with a choice of two models which, incidentally, were available in just one colour—blue-grey. There was either a 'limousine' or a 'cabrio limousine' (with a roll-back, canvas sunshine-roof) costing an extra 60 Reichsmark.

A contract for the supply of a car could be made at any of the National Socialist cooperative centres where the necessary forms were to be completed and signed personally; in the case of a woman the signature of the husband had to be obtained. The savings scheme itself required the saver to commit themselves to the purchase of at least 5 Reichsmark worth of saving-stamps per week, to be affixed in a savings book which had to be exchanged for a new one when completed. The saver was also entitled to purchase more stamps at any one time, even up to the full value of the car. There was a reduced savings plan for young persons and those on low incomes which could be increased when incomes rose.

Each car was automatically insured third party and part comprehensive for a period of two years, which was inclusive in the scheme at an

A Type 38 Versuchswagen (trial car), heading out on one of the many promotional trips for the Volkswagen savings scheme. Length is now 4,200mm (13.8ft), and width and height are 1,550mm (4.9ft).

extra cost of 200 Reichsmark, bringing the total outlay up to 1,190 Reichsmark.

The contract could not be cancelled except by losing all that had already been paid in, and any default, of even one payment, rendered a breach of contract and the risk of forfeiting all he or she had paid in. Probably the worst aspect of the scheme, was the lack of interest on the savings, which would require a period of well in excess of four years at minimum weekly payments before completion. Altogether, a total of 336,668 Germans put their name to this scheme, which led to the accumulation of a total of 280 million Reichsmark. It has always been suspected that the whole thing was a giant con-trick, possibly to help raise funds for military purposes. Surprisingly, this was not the case for, in fact, every last *Pfennig* was deposited by the KDF in the Bank of German Labour in Berlin—which was seized by the Russians at the end of the war.

One can only have compassion for the multitude of hopefuls who had placed their trust in this scheme in the hope of achieving what to many was a life's ambition, however naïve they may seem to us today. (For an account of the long-drawn-out legal battle between the savers and the Volkswagen company, which began in 1949, when the factory was back in German hands, see Chapter 5.)

On 6 September 1938 Porsche received the German national prize for his services as an engineer, in particular for presenting Germany with its people's car. It was handed over by Hitler in a ceremony at the Chancellery. Hitler always showed his favouritism towards Porsche, even in public, despite the fact that Porsche never wore uniform. Ghislaine Kaes remembers that it was Porsche's strength of personality and refusal to put on airs and graces, along with his unmodified Austrian accent, which seemed to attract Hitler. In 1939, the Association of German Engineers presented Porsche with the Grashoff Memorial Medal and on 12 September 1940 Porsche was made an honorary professor by the Reichsminister of Science and Education.

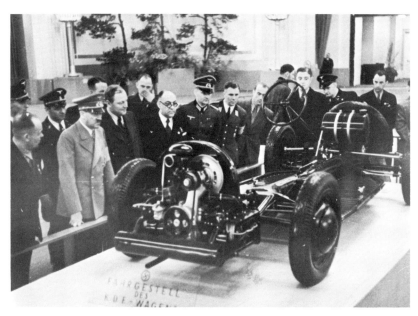

Surrounded by Nazi top-brass, Hitler stops to admire a well-polished KDF chassis at the 1939 Berlin Motor Show.

The 1939 Berlin Motor Show held on 16 February was to see the Volkswagen prominently displayed, much to the elation of Hitler, and accompanied by an entourage of Nazi brass hats and dignitaries. Porsche's masterpiece was now officially known as the KDF Wagen, but the name never did catch on with the general public, who continued to call it the Volkswagen. As a further propaganda measure, Hitler ordered 200,000 Reichsmark to be set aside to cover promotional journeys throughout Germany. These were a resounding success, attracting crowds wherever they halted and undoubtedly sending many an over-enthusiastic spectator scurrying off to sign up for one of the cars.

By late 1938, the war clouds were once again gathering over Europe. Hitler's annexation of Austria, followed by the march into the Sudetenland and the invasion of all Czechoslovakia, placed the writing firmly on the wall, and World War II was but a short time away. The hopes of millions of civilians of having their own car soon began to fade for it was the car's military application which was to take precedence and only two hundred KDF cars were produced by the time war broke out. These, along with military prototypes, were built in Porsche's Volkswagen engineering works housed beneath the offices at 2 Spitalwaldstrasse, an operation which was transferred to the KDF factory early in 1940. These few KDF cars became the prized possessions of the Nazi hierarchy.

As mentioned earlier, it was the military who, right from the beginning, showed the keenest interest in Porsche's scheme, and in 1937 a cross-country car consisting of a cut-down Beetle, akin in a remote way to the modern Beetle beach buggy, made its appearance. This design later evolved into a small jeep, followed by a larger jeep—a prototype of the 'Kübelwagen'. This design, which was called Type 62, featured a lightweight jeep body built by Ambi Budd Corporation of Berlin, a part-owned American subsidiary, fitted to a Volkswagen chassis. The Kübelwagen passed its preliminary testing in Afghanistan with flying colours and the air-cooled engine was to prove ideal, not only in the severe heat of the north African desert, but also in the sub-zero temperatures of the Russian front. Field-Marshal Rommel was particularly complimentary about them, saying to Porsche:

Your jeep, which I used in North Africa, saved my life. It didn't pack up when crossing a minefield, when the heavy Horsch trucks travelling behind with the supplies were blown sky high.

Whether Rommel was just lucky and did not hit a mine is not clear!

The massive car factory, fully equipped with up-to-date machinery, some of which was purchased by Porsche from the United States during his visit in 1937, must have appeared right from the outset as the perfect war plant, set well away from the eastern front, and clear of any prime bombing target. But only a small percentage of the plant's full potential was ever utilised for manufacturing cars; instead the war effort asked for aeroplane repairs. A total of 66,285 vehicles were produced from 1940 to the early part of 1945.

Hebmüller was one of the firms that produced cabriolet models. This one, built in the late 1940s and now preserved in the Wolfsburg museum, bears a marked resemblance to the one-off Type 15 two-seater roadster built at the factory in 1946. Hebmüller made 750 such models.

A parade of KDFs near the Brandenburg Gate in Berlin where, on 23 June 1939, Hitler demonstrated his Volkswagen to the world press, no doubt with a more peaceful invasion in mind. Had it not been for the war (as a report compiled by the British in 1946 readily admitted) the KDF would undoubtedly have made quite an impact on the world's markets. In fact, only 630 KDF civilian cars were built during the war—accounting for only 1 per cent of total production—and they went exclusively to Nazi officials.

By the outbreak of war Porsche found himself fully occupied with a never-ending list of military requirements, including numerous tank designs, aero engines and a wide variety of vehicles not only designed to transport Hitler's armies across conquered territories but also to ensure their full mobility in the most extreme conditions.

Amongst the mountain of other orders was Type 83, an automatic gearbox for the VW, Type 107, a gas turbine power unit for the VW, and Type 115, a supercharged VW engine, and even a VW diesel engine. Nevertheless, he still found time for his pet project. As well as the

85

By 1939 the cross-country car had developed into a small jeep with canvas doors.

The next stage was the Type 62 Kübelwagen prototype, seen here in late 1939 at the Spitalwaldstrasse works where all the military prototypes were built.

The fully evolved Type 82 production model Kübelwagen, with the spare wheel now positioned on top of the front hood.

people's car, there was the people's tractor powered by a vw-type engine, along with more unusual projects such as wind machines. Porsche, in complete contrast to a few years previously, had state finance readily available for all his projects.

He spent the war years commuting between the factory, manned almost entirely by prisoners of war and other forced-labour contingents from Nazi occupied countries, and his offices in Stuttgart. He became extremely distressed by the plight of these wretched individuals, whose meagre rations left them grossly undernourished, not to mention the harsh treatment they received from the SS guards. So outraged was Porsche that he went to Hitler and pointed out that he could not be expected to maintain an efficient workforce whilst men were starving to death and living in a state of utter deprivation. Had it been anyone other than Hitler's favourite designer, Porsche might well have found himself

The first of the amphibians, a Type 128 prototype Schwimmwagen, distinguishable from the production model by its more angular appearance.

The Type 166 production model Schwimmwagen, seen here with the propeller in the up position ready for road travel.

These Kübelwagens, nearing the end of the production line, later saw active service as far south as Africa and as far north as Scandinavia, not to mention the punishing ordeals of the Russian front.

in serious trouble for making such an approach to the Führer, but, as it was, Hitler swallowed Porsche's plausible excuse for improving the prisoner's lot, and his pleas were met with extra allocations of food and a few other essential items.

In 1942, Porsche came up with the answer to a request from the Wehrmacht for an amphibious jeep—Type 166, the 'Schwimmwagen', powered by the larger 1,131cc engine—which was introduced into the Kübelwagen range in the same year and superseded the 995cc engine in all vws after that. The Schwimmwagen had five forward gears and four-wheel drive. A variety of offshoots came from these two main models, which made up the bulk of wartime production at the KDF factory. The Beetle continued to exist in military guise, as Type 82E, a Beetle body fitted to the Kübelwagen chassis, and Type 87 'Kommandeurwagen', again using the Beetle body, this time fitted to the Schwimmwagen chassis, and virtually the only type of Beetle ever produced with four-wheel drive.

Designed to tackle the most obstinate of conditions. Shown here is a Type 155 Schneeraupe (snow caterpillar), a Kübelwagen rigged out with rear caterpillars. Models such as this were only ever produced in small numbers.

The 'go-anywhere' jeep—a Schwimmwagen with bolt-on paddles to aid traction on mud and in snow.

'The one that got away'—the Type 87 Kommandeurwagen, based on the prototype Schwimmwagen chassis and virtually the only type of four-wheel drive Beetle ever built. Only a few were made, at the Spitalwaldstrasse works, and it never went into production. The Type 82E Beetle based on the Kübelwagen chassis was identical in appearance to it and 564 of these military Beetles were built during the war.

The end of the war was preceded by intense bombing of the factory which, by that time, was being used for the limited manufacture of airframes, mines and, reportedly, components for the V1 and V2 rockets (which may have been the cause of the bombing). Porsche ordered the removal of some machinery to the cellars, where production continued in relative safety, whilst other machinery was removed to sites in the surrounding area. Work continued piecemeal in small works set well away from the main plant. Rumour had it that, in order to create an impression of greater damage than had actually been inflicted, German sappers would throw grenades into the plant after an air raid, but these stories are now considered to be without foundation by vw people at Wolfsburg.

By early 1945, production at the heavily damaged plant gradually

Fuel shortages lead to a number of special conversions. This is a model called the 'Holzbrenner', or wood burner, with an engine converted to run on carbon monoxide. This was produced from a stove heated from underneath located under the front hood. The performance of the car was however severely reduced.

ground to a standstill, by which time Porsche had been evacuated to Austria, leaving to the conquerors the fate of Hitler's Strength-Through-Joy factory, where he had laid the foundation stone a mere six years previously.

This bulbous-nosed Type 82E, introduced in 1944, was the 'Holzkohlengas' car, with an engine converted to run on wood or coal. The required fuels are stored on the roof.

4

From Out of the Ashes

The fall of the Third Reich had turned Germany into a no-man's land where anything and everything became the spoils of war. The giant industrial showpiece built by Hitler to fulfil the dreams of a nation had in the greater part been reduced to rubble and twisted metal, with some two thirds of the original production shops totally devastated by the daylight bombing raids. Estimates for war damage totalled a staggering 156 million Reichsmark.

Despite the extensive damage inflicted on the mammoth building, one part had survived the massive aerial bombardment; that part which formed the very heart of the factory—the giant power plant whose two enormous turbine generators provided the total electricity and heating requirements of the plant and town. This too would have died along with the rest save for a handful of dedicated engineers who remained at their posts, keeping the vital machinery operating and in working order on reduced power when the rest of the factory was abandoned. The foresight and presence of mind of these individuals was the major factor in the survival of the factory.

The Americans were soon replaced by the British, who took over the plant in the spring of 1945 under the Allied plan to divide Germany into four separate Occupation zones. One of the first moves made by the British was the appointment of an embryo town council who, at their first meeting, officially named the town Wolfsburg.

Amongst the first British troops to be garrisoned at Wolfsburg was a squadron of an armoured regiment who had already handed in their tanks, plus a contingent of the Pioneer Corps. The latter, whilst stationed in the town, provided a guard at the factory gates during the removal of German army material manufactured at the plant during the war. Their main task was the staffing of the displaced persons camps, which involved the repatriation and subsequent movement of the wartime foreign labour from all parts of the British Occupation zone.

Colonel M. A. McEvoy CBE, responsible at British army headquarters for organising the branch of REME (Royal Electrical and Mechanical Engineers) dealing with repairs to civilian vehicles in order to get some road transport moving, remembered the former KDF Wagen (Volkswagen) factory near Fallersleben; he looked at the map, confirmed that the factory lay within the British zone, and saw the potential of producing Kübelwagens or even the KDF Wagen, as light transportation for the British Occupation forces.

Before the war, McEvoy, a consultant engineer, had visited the Berlin motor show with British members of the press, where he was impressed with Porsche's people's car. The result was that a REME detachment was put into the Wolfsburg factory.

Having established a repair shop in an area of the plant which had escaped severe damage from bombing, this attachment, which utilised the remnants of the German wartime staff, including several heads of departments who had remained at the factory after the cessation of hostilities, was given the task of overhauling civilian trucks and buses, with the Volkswagenwerk Company acting as contractors to REME. To meet overheads and wages for the German workforce, repairs to vehicles were invoiced by the company and after being certified by the British authorities at the factory these invoices were forwarded to the German civil authorities at Lüneburg for reimbursement out of 'Occupation costs'.

Naturally the costs involved in the running of a heavily damaged plant like the Wolfsburg factory (including temporary repairs, bought-out parts and essential equipment) were considerable and in order to provide the necessary working capital the Property Control branch of the Military Government arranged a loan from one of Germany's big banks in order to get things moving.

Although the civilian vehicle-repair function was the responsibility of the army until the end of 1945, civil affairs proper, including any production of vehicles, were the responsibility of Military Government.

This led to the installation of a Military Government resident engineering officer to take overall charge of the factory and in August 1945 Major Ivan Hirst took up residence at Wolfsburg.

As will be seen, some of the information in this chapter was obtained during a meeting with Ivan Hirst, arranged through REME headquarters at Arborfield.

Trained as an optical engineer before the war, Hirst had joined the Territorial Army and by the outbreak of war he had reached the rank of captain. Transferred to REME in 1942, he became second in command, equivalent to works manager, of a British tank overhaul workshop which later in the war used a factory at Brussels and largely employed civilian labour. When the idea of building VWs was first discussed, Hirst was transferred to Military Government, in order to take charge of the Wolfsburg factory.

Military Government, or 'Mil Gov' as it was known in the field, was virtually synonymous with Control Commission for Germany (CCG). Mil Gov/CCG personnel were a blend of British and Canadian army, airforce and naval personnel, many of whom were lawyers, accountants, engineers and so on in civilian life, plus a number of civilian officials from the UK. Some of the military became civilians at a later date—sometimes even in the same job in Germany, as was the case with Ivan Hirst in the winter of 1946-7.

Field-Marshal Montgomery had originally opposed a large influx of civilian CCG officials to Germany, pointing out that he already possessed perfectly adequate personnel amongst the armed forces (officers whose previous occupations qualified them for the task), which resulted in a compromise, with Mil Gov on the ground (wartime soldiers) and a hierarchy largely staffed by civilians.

When discussing the role played by the British Army's REME detachment at the factory, as distinct from that of Military Government, and the Control Commission, Ivan Hirst recalls that its outstanding contribution to VW was that it served to hold together a few key German personnel who might otherwise have dispersed in the confusion and turmoil which reigned in 1945.

REME's role at the factory after this date, when its initial task of repairs to civilian trucks and buses was phased out and handed back to the civilian motor trade, was supervising the repair and overhaul of Volkswagens used by the Occupation authorities after 1945, when production proper got under way. Alongside the aforementioned tasks, they also arranged the rebuilding of army jeep engines by vw, which continued until the latter part of 1947. By 1948 the entire vw overhaul operation had passed to the company, with REME in the background as customers' representatives.

As the senior Mil Gov officer on the industry side, Hirst reported directly to Colonel C. R. Radclyffe CBE DSO at CCG headquarters at Minden, who was in charge of all light mechanical-engineering industry in the British zone.

Originally a career officer before World War I, Radclyffe had left the army in the 'twenties to go to the USA where he entered the motor industry, but later returned to the UK where he rejoined the army in 1939. Although he died in 1949 he had played a major part in reviving the vw concern under British auspices. He was described by Ivan Hirst as a pillar of strength. On his regular monthly visits to the factory he gave much sound advice and even today he is still held in high regard by those who worked under him during those early post-war years.

The utterly miserable state of affairs which existed at Wolfsburg in those early post-war days (and elsewhere in Germany come to that matter) can best be judged from Hirst's personal recollections of the situation which confronted him on his arrival in mid-1945.

When first sent to Wolfsburg, I had no specific briefing; I was simply told to take charge of the factory, vw production at that time being a vague possibility. Germany had collapsed. German morale was at a very low ebb. All German cities and large towns had been devastated; we'd seen nothing like it in the UK, France or Belgium. Industry was a wreck, the railways were barely operating, civilian road transport was at a standstill, many bridges were blown up (with Bailey bridges at key crossings).

I came to Wolfsburg on a Sunday afternoon, and drove straight to the factory. Though obviously heavily damaged, it was an impressive sight, a monument to the Nazi party. Then I drove into the town, which had remained undamaged, but a strange place, because the initial building programme, which consisted in the main of flats, had been halted early in

97

the war, leaving unfinished streets leading into open heathland. Most of the hutted camps, built during the war for the foreign workers employed by vw, were occupied by other foreign workers ('displaced persons') awaiting repatriation to Eastern Europe from all parts of the British zone. [Being near to the border of the Russian zone, now East Germany, and being connected by rail to the east as well as the rest of Germany, Wolfsburg, with its extensive hutted accommodation, undamaged by bombing, proved an ideal transit camp for Eastern European forced labour from the British zone.]

Next morning at the factory, I met the remaining top management, and in particular Rudolph Brörmann, who had been chief inspector under Professor Porsche during the war, and had been made plant manager by the us authorities at the end of the war.

We went round the factory. The power station, a big plant with 60MW installed capacity, was still intact and running but desperately short of coal; neither the factory nor the town was connected to the British-zone grid. (The power station had been connected to the national grid at a point in the Russian zone, but the authorities there were not prepared to send any coal to Wolfsburg.)

The roof of the press-shop building was off, leaving the presses open to the elements. The building intended for car assembly (which was used during the war for aircraft repair) was heavily damaged, with the roof down and holes in the floors. The building equipped as machine shops was likewise heavily damaged. Only the fourth building, intended as materials-testing laboratories, parts stores etc, remained sufficiently intact to be usable, and it was here that the truck- and bus-repair operations were carried out under the directions of REME.

The ground along the factory front had been churned up by the bombing. Some of the factory dining halls had survived, but food was minimal.

One consolation was the fact that a much smaller factory (Vorwerk) at nearby Brunswick (Braunschweig), equipped as toolrooms, had remained undamaged and skilled craftsmen were still available.

The small German workforce who had remained at the factory after the war—a number of those employed at Wolfsburg during the war years had been arrested on various charges—were suffering from utter dejection and deprivation. Morale, which had just about reached rock bottom, was well reflected by the state of basic amenities such as the toilets, which, as Hirst recalls, were filthy, with the plumbing having

An early Type 11 being lowered on to its chassis by former German prisoners of war—still sporting tank caps.

been damaged during the air raids and no attempt whatsoever having been made to carry out repairs (and it was a very hot summer).

Food, of course, was at a premium, with the majority of the population existing on a diet of little more than potatoes and whatever else could be scrounged on the black market. A harrowing incident recalled by Hirst took place one night directly outside his bedroom window, when the owner of a kitchen garden murdered a man for stealing a few potatoes: a sharp reminder of the desperate plight which faced this demoralised nation of people just after the war.

In order to arrive at a decision as to the feasibility of restarting car production, Hirst along with Brörmann and his staff carried out a general assessment of the plant and the availability of materials.

The Kübelwagen bodies which had been made during the war by Ambi Budd in Berlin were now in short supply, with spasmodic train loads of complete bodies still continuing to arrive at the factory. (These were finished in the old desert colour—yellow—two years after Rommel's era!) However, partly due to the difficulty of direct communication with the Russian officials in Berlin, and also because it was known that the Ambi Budd plant had been largely destroyed, it was clear they could not rely on Ambi Budd for post-war production. All hinged on the feasibility of bringing the Beetle body into production at Wolfsburg.

A number of Kübelwagen and Schwimmwagen had been put together by the German staff shortly after the British moved into the plant from stocks of parts left over from the war period. The Schwimmwagen proved a particular favourite with certain high-spirited army officers in the early days, who were reported to have used them on the Mittelland canal, racing them straight off the bank and into the water as a demonstration for visitors to the factory.

The machining lines and assembly lines for engine and transmission units were still in the factory cellars and at dispersal sites in the countryside around Wolfsburg, and also at two bigger sites at Gifhorn and Lüneburg, where they had been moved in anticipation of the air attack. Some previous accounts, suggesting that the majority of the machinery had either been severely damaged or smashed beyond repair, are in fact untrue, for the majority had survived. The foundry building, intended as an iron foundry when it was completed in 1939, had never been equipped and this, as will be explained later, was brought into use as a light-metal foundry.

From the general assessment by the German executives under Hirst's direction it became clear that if materials and components could be obtained, it would be possible to get the Beetle into production.

Although the military version of the VW (the Kübelwagen) was not unfamiliar to the British as many had been captured during the war, the civilian saloon, or KDF Wagen, was virtually unknown. In order to supply a 'demonstrator', a pre-war KDF Wagen left in the factory for repair by a German owner was comandeered, sprayed army green and sent to army HQ for assessment and, as Ivan Hirst recalls, '. . . the vague thinking there crystallised into a decision, whereupon an order for 10,000 saloons was placed upon VW, to supply the British army and other British agencies in Germany. This was the green light for Beetle production.' There were already smaller orders in hand for runs of the 'Beetle vans' for the Reichpost when Hirst arrived in Wolfsburg, but scarcely production in the full sense—merely assembly of parts left over from wartime production, plus some manufacturing of body panels and the like from steel sheets also left over.

The 'Beetle van' was in fact a re-hash of the old Type 88 'Model B' van, built during KDF days by Porsche, renumbered Type 83 on the new post-war production list.

From the general assessment of the situation at the factory, plus estimates of availabilities of materials and bought-out components (such as sheet steel, forgings, glass, castings, electrics, cloth, carburettors, fuel pumps, clutches, dampers, tyres, batteries, etc), the German executives proposed a production rate of 1,000 cars per month, to be reached early in 1946. This plan was accepted and the achievement of 1,000 cars per month by March 1946 was publicised widely in CCG headquarters where the goodwill of other branches was needed to get their support—for example, glass was at a premium and all allocations were a matter for the CCG branch dealing with building materials, with the emphasis on housing rather than industry (because of the massive number of people made homeless during the wartime bombing). It is also worth remembering that the German economy was a vacuum at that time, with scarcely any factories operating. Virtually no other car manufacturer started up until a much later date.

Orders for the above-mentioned materials and bought-out components were sent out to the industry's usual suppliers, but with no results. Based on the knowledge that the supply firms in question were either completely out of action, or so disorganised that they could not fulfil the orders, Hirst arranged for a schedule of requirements, containing a breakdown of suppliers according to their various districts in the British zone, to be sent to CCG HQ at Minden, who in turn sent down instructions to individual officers in charge of the various districts to get suppliers' factories reactivated (gas, electricity, labour, repairs, etc).

Preparations for production included the arduous task of clearing vast amounts of war debris and the fixing up of temporary shelters over the production area. This was achieved by rigging up poles (pine-tree trunks) with sheeting over the top, which at least provided some sort of protection whilst proper roof repairs were got under way. After this, in late 1945 and early 1946, the machine tools from the dispersal sites and the cellars were re-installed.

Coal supplies remained precarious until the factory power station was connected up to the British-zone grid, which allowed the power station to run at full capacity and thus qualify for allocations of coal, previously 'scrounged' or begged from a British team in charge of some lignite fields (lignite being soft brown coal) at nearby Helmstedt.

The presses were found to be in need of relatively minor repairs and luckily, all the press tools for the KDF Wagen bodies were still at Wolfsburg, together with those used during the war for the chassis frame (basically the same as that of the Kübelwagen).

Although arrangements were in hand for buying out certain components, others would have to be produced at the factory, such as carburettors, fuel pumps, dampers and clutch assemblies, as they were just not available elsewhere. A light-alloy foundry had to be opened up for the production of crankcase and transmission housings and steering boxes. Unfortunately the branch of CCG had closed down the foundries which had originally supplied the factory since they were classified as part of the aircraft industry which was destined to be completely dismantled, but, as Hirst explained, the dies were rescued in the nick of time. The foundry at Wolfsburg was an empty shell, having never been equipped for production, and this required equipping before entering service.

vw production in 1945, whilst the plant was in the process of being re-equipped and reorganised, and outside suppliers were being re-activated, was an *ad hoc* affair, making do with whatever was available from old stocks. The first Beetle bodies were produced from existing stocks of steel sheets which, incidentally, presented a problem where the roof panel was concerned since sufficiently large sheets were not available. As a temporary measure, while awaiting a new butt welder (built at the toolrooms at Brunswick) two smaller pressings were crudely

Wolfsburg's test track being used by the British to put the Type 51s through their paces—a far cry from the ultra modern complex completed in the early 'seventies.

lap-welded together to keep production moving until larger sheets could be obtained. As this was a dubious means of construction, a number of these cars which had the lap-welded seam running across the roof from the door pillars on either side were deliberately rolled over to test the strength of the roof.

The 1945 vws and a few in the early part of 1946 were designated Type 51. The dies for producing the front-axle forgings for the KDF saloon had been lost in Silesia during the latter part of the war. There was, however, a stock of Kübelwagen front-axle forgings still available, plus stocks of the reduction gears which had been fitted to the outer ends of the Kübelwagen's swing axles at the rear. Until the new Beetle-type forgings could be obtained these early post-war Beetles were fitted with the Kübelwagen parts, which gave them an unusually high ground clearance and an appearance very similar to the wartime Type 82E, which prompted Gordon Wilkins in an article on the Type 51 in *Motor*

An impressive line-up of Type 53s, parked with military precision along the southern frontage of the factory in 1945.

magazine for May 1946 to describe the car as looking like a Beetle on stilts, probably made to look even more odd by the use of Kübelwagen headlamps fitted on the earlier cars into the somewhat larger Beetle lamp housings.

Accounts of hand tooling during the British phase at the factory were described by Hirst as 'nonsense', and he went on to say:

> By and large, all the presses and press tools and all the machinery and tooling had survived the war, although they were dispersed and some were in a sorry state, with gaps where items *had* been destroyed during the war. The cars delivered in the winter of 1945-6 were made using this machinery and tooling, though the overhead conveyors were out of action.

The gaps had to be filled, in particular by making new body jigs (which *had* fallen victim to the bombing), a task carried out by the vw people themselves. (During the British phase, a number of specialist teams and various experts visited the plant from time to time and whilst there they were able to give the factory the benefit of their expertise.) Hirst added that more modern processes, such as bonderising and dip-painting of the body shells, were subsequently introduced, before the British handed over the factory to the German authorities.

In order to bring in supplies of raw materials and car components before the railways were running normally, the factory acquired a number of civilian trucks. They also obtained a number of buses to bring in labour from surrounding villages—an illustration of the acute manpower and housing shortage plaguing the factory at that time.

As the wartime labour force had consisted largely of foreign nationals who had been repatriated shortly after the cessation of hostilities, it was necessary to call upon the services of the manpower division of Military Government, who, among other measures, arranged for German ex-soldiers being discharged from prisoner-of-war camps to be offered work at the Wolfsburg factory.

In order to house the new labour, derelict and vandalised camps were renovated, with the German personnel manager taking on the task of looking after the needs of the occupants. REME personnel were housed in what had previously been bachelor accommodation at Steimkeberg, a suburb of Wolfsburg. The officers, including Ivan Hirst and his Mil

Gov colleagues, lived in what had been the company's guest house in the town.

Rapid turnover of labour was a serious problem, as the new men often left as soon as they found their families and could set up house elsewhere, but many did stay and some are still with the company today.

When discussing the subject of relations between the British officers and the German workforce in general at that time, Hirst summed them up as being warm, although he said that at first there was naturally some caginess on both sides (bearing in mind that the two countries had been at war only a matter of months previously!), but both sides had a job to do, and they needed one another.

In connection with labour relations at that time, Ivan Hirst recalls: 'As a channel of communication between the labour force, the management and ourselves, I obtained authority to hold elections for a works council, before German assemblies of any kind—not to mention trade unions—were allowed.'

Manpower problems were not restricted to the factory floor. Management was described as being like a game of musical chairs, a situation brought about by the process of de-Nazification. Many people in top and middle management and in other key jobs had to be dismissed on political grounds (the usual charge was that of being a member of the Nazi party), with vacancies being filled by recruitment, which entailed many time-consuming interviews and discussions. Often these de-Nazification decisions were reversed on appeal, only to be reversed again at a later date, all in all creating a considerable extra burden for the British and for the German top management.

By 1947 the position with regard to departmental heads had become more stable. The new works manager, appointed by Military Government, was Herr Steinmeyer who stayed in the job until his retirement years later. His assistant was Dr Otto Höhne, who succeeded him and was the top production man at Wolfsburg until he in turn retired some three years ago. Other senior executives appointed from outside, or promoted or confirmed in office while VW was under Military Government included Paulsen (purchasing), Dr Feuereisen (sales and service), Goransch (personnel), Hiemenz (finance) and Orlich (inspection); all of these managers continued in their respective jobs until they retired or died.

Theft also proved a problem. The period 1945-6 was a lawless time in Germany. Because of the dire shortages of even the most basic items that created such deprivation and hardship amongst the community at large, many who would otherwise have been honest were tempted to steal and this led to the disappearance of many items from the factory, including car components and virtually anything which could be carried away, some of which found their way on to the black market.

With the help of the Mil Gov public safety branch, Hirst arranged for a works police force to be set up in late 1945. Made up of German nationals, the factory police received their training under regular German police at Lüneburg (equivalent of the county town) under the direction of British police officers. One point of interest is the cap which is still worn today; it was modelled on Ivan Hirst's service dress cap, way back in 1945.

There was a dark shadow over the Volkswagen company in the first few years after the war—the threat of dismantling for reparations. Installations which had been built specifically as war plants were made available to the Allies as reparations, and were automatically destined for dismantling. Since the Wolfsburg factory had originally and quite genuinely been built for civilian production, it was not classified as a 'war plant' to be automatically dismantled. (Like all the German car factories it had of course produced a considerable quantity of military vehicles and also a fairly wide range of other military equipment during the war period, although its production capacity for cars had not been fully utilised.) Nonetheless, because it had not existed prior to 1938, it was listed as surplus to the 'post-war level of industry', a ceiling which the Allies imposed on Germany, and it was therefore still available for reparations, ie, any of the Allies could bid for it. But (and this is the factor which saved the factory from an ignominious end) because the British and other Allied authorities needed vw cars while in occupation, a four-year reserve was placed on the factory in 1945 and before these four years elapsed the level-of-industry plan had been scrapped.

Being ex-Nazi party property, the vw factory (renamed the Wolfsburg

107

Motor Works in late 1945 as this was then more acceptable to the British authorities than the original pre-war name) was brought under 'Property Control'. The prime function of Property Control was to look after the assets of individuals who had left Germany, but it was extended to include the task of sorting out the ownership of ex-Nazi party (DAF) properties, including the vw factory and the town of Wolfsburg, which formed part of the original Volkswagenwerk scheme. This task fell to Leslie Barber from CCG headquarters in late 1945.

On Hirst's suggestion, accepted by Barber (described by Hirst as an excellent man), it was agreed that a CCG board for the vw organisation should be set up. This acted initially as a forum for discussing all aspects of the Volkswagenwerk organisation, and was in effect a British board of directors for the ownerless company till September 1949, when the factory was officially handed over to the German authorities.

The chairmanship of the board alternated between Colonel Radclyffe and Barber till Barber returned home, after which Radclyffe took over as permanent chairman until September 1949.

The first full-time 'Property Control Officer' at Wolfsburg, was Major Alistair McInnes, a Scottish accountant, and Hirst recalls that McInnes did an excellent job and generally helped out with vw matters. As well as factory administration, McInnes was also responsible for the Wolfsburg housing. Other than Ivan Hirst, Alistair McInnes, today a church minister living in Scotland, is probably the only surviving senior officer still living in Britain today who served at the factory at that time. Both he and Ivan Hirst were then very young men, still in their early thirties, but they did much to keep things going at that highly critical period. After humorously claiming to have been put in charge of the purse strings because he was a Scotsman, McInnes went on to recall how he came to be at Wolfsburg.

When fighting was over in Belgium, I was called to rear HQ 21 army group for an interview with a brigadier. Before I had joined the army, I had completed my studies for the final examination of the Chartered Institute of Secretaries, and during the war I studied accountancy. Although the brigadier had all the relevant information about me he asked about my civilian work, my studies, my service career and my attitude to various other matters. Finally he asked, 'If we sent you to the Opel car factory, do you think you could organise it?.' As I was going riding and didn't wish to prolong the interview and, in any case, I thought he was joking, I said, 'Yes, of course.' The interview ended rather abruptly, and I heard nothing more of the matter. I was posted to Hildesheim as a Property Control Officer with Military Government and I was perfectly happy there. At the beginning of September 1945 I received a signal to report at Volkswagen-werk and take charge of the commercial organisation and administration. During a quick 'recce' of the factory I met Major Ivan Hirst who was just going off on a well-deserved leave to the UK. When I took up my duties a few days later, I was paralysed with fear due to the size of the place, and yet I had had no briefing on my responsibilities or my duties. All I knew was that my work came under the control of the Property Control Division of Military Government/Control Commission in Berlin, and my chief would be Mr Barber of the CCG. Within a couple of days he came to the factory to tell me what it was all about. I was given a free hand, told to get on with it, but if I had any problems to let him know.

When Major Hirst returned from leave, we got down to details. He was in overall charge but anything on the commercial side was my absolute responsibility, and anything on the engineering or production side was his. Both our jobs impinged on each other all the time, so it was a matter of co-operation all the time. It was imperative to both of us that the factory got off the ground as quickly as possible and there were so many problems that had to be solved as they arose. Often we had to work into the small hours to get things moving. We agreed we would not work on a Saturday afternoon or Sunday unless it was absolutely essential. It was a good decision for, while we were both young, we could not have kept up the pressure of that kind seven days a week. There were many occasions when we did not get our weekend off, but it was usually worth it!

In order to help out on the administration side, Mil Gov in the summer of 1945 furnished Hirst with an assistant, an army major who looked after personnel problems, as well as helping out with administrative duties. He was soon replaced by R. H. Berryman OBE, a wartime wing commander, who had joined CCG as a civilian official in a less senior grade. He did not much care for administrative matters and so it was agreed that he would work as Hirst's deputy on the production side. Having regard to the many problems to be faced at that time, including those created by the de-Nazification process and the start up of production, Berryman, as Hirst recalls, was a first-class trouble-shooter on the factory floor, at a time when vw management was at its weakest. During his stay at the plant, he made a substantial contribution and helped to get production under way.

It must be stressed, however, that the task of putting the factory back on its feet and getting Beetle production started was accomplished by team effort, German as well as British. This is Hirst's view, and McInnes likewise stresses the enthusiasm shown by the Germans at Wolfsburg, and the hard work done by everyone, managers and blue-collar workers alike, under extraordinary difficult conditions.

Stories about the vw concern being offered to the British car industry appear to be without foundation. According to Ivan Hirst the factory was never actually offered to anyone. Australia was the only country to show any real interest and this soon diminished when the visiting team realised that vw would be working for the Allies for some time to come.

The American Ford motor company showed a vague interest (despite the fact that the plant was not officially on offer) but due more to the geographical location than the actual potential of the factory as a car-producing plant they soon lost interest. Ford is reputed to have said that the plant was not worth a damn.

Sir William Rootes (later Lord Rootes) went to Wolfsburg in search of a big die-sinking machine which, if it had not been destroyed by a direct hit in the bombing, would have been requisitioned for use in Britain. After spending a day looking round the plant, he turned to Hirst and said, 'If you think you're going to get that car back into production, then you're a bloody fool.'

As it was to be expected, during the start-up period many problems came to light, and these had to be overcome without delay. The stock of carburettors originally made by the Berlin Solex factory quickly ran out and the factory had to produce their own. Although the car-burettor body and float chamber did not present too big a problem, as these could be made by vw themselves, the smaller parts such as needle valves, floats and jets were a different proposition. It was a German camera firm who came to the rescue, for when Hirst and Brörmann discussed the problem, it was evident to the British officer, originally an instrument engineer himself, that one of the camera firms in nearby

Brunswick would be able to produce the smaller parts. Until carburettors could once more be obtained from Solex, the Beetle was fitted with the Wolfsburg 'pirate' brand, which Hirst said proved satisfactory and kept things going until Solex in Paris developed a new carb for the Beetle late in 1947.

One perhaps humorous example of these problems which held up car deliveries for a brief period was a delay in the arrival of fan belts from Conti of Hanover. The driving belt in a fridge is similar to that of a car fan belt, and this led to a consignment which was originally destined for Wolfsburg going to the German Fridgidaire factory instead!

Steering faults were far more serious. Whether actually through steering failure, or through over exuberance on the part of drivers, a number of fatal accidents took place during 1946 involving British officers. The story behind these early defects was explained in some detail by Ivan Hirst.

> To economise on non-ferrous metals, the steering-box cover had been changed during the war to one of pressed steel. The original cover had the boss for the adjusting screw as part of the casting on the underside, so that it prevented the steering nut lifting out of engagement with the worm in the event of the adjusting screw coming out, as it could do if its lock nut was not tightened properly. There was a design error in the replacement pressed-steel covers and there was no longer any 'fail safe' internal protrusion to prevent disengagement of the adjusting screw. There was, of course, a strong helical spring associated with the worm and nut, but in the conditions prevailing in 1945-6, these often broke. With a slack adjusting screw and a broken spring, when the car went over a pothole at speed (and there were plenty to choose from at that time) the steering wheel could become disconnected from the front wheels. When the defect was identified, cars already in service were quickly modified by users' own repair shops by simply fitting washers on the drop-arm shaft, between the drop arm and the underside of the steering box, to perform the same function as the boss on the underside of the original cast cover.

He went on to explain another, possibly less serious, steering fault.

> Steel was tightly rationed at that time and, rather than waste precious supplies in the form of imperfect forgings (in this case, steering arms) the supplier in question was reheating cracked forgings and restriking them to

Even the Kübelwagen was pressed into service to fill a need when other
manufacturers were bombed out of business.

hide the crack! We satisfied ourselves that there was no criminal intent,
just shockingly bad judgement on the part of a foreman at the suppliers'
works.

It is unlikely that this particular fault caused any fatalities, as the
breakage of one steering arm does not result in total loss of steering on
the Beetle.

A total of 2,490 vws were produced in 1945, including 703 type 51s
and 58 type IIs, with a workforce which, by the end of that year, had
grown to 6,000. Many of these were occupied on non-productive work,
such as clearing up the hundreds of tons of war debris strewn throughout the factory and cutting down steel girders, hanging wires, and the
added hazard of falling masonry.

With roof repairs still in the initial stages, working conditions during

The special two-seater roadster of 1946. As an economy measure the front-hood pressing doubles as an engine lid, giving it that 'coming-or-going' appearance. The polished nipple hub-caps are the same as those later fitted to the first export models.

that first winter were appalling, with everyday working life very much dependent on the weather. Taking into account the lack of basic amenities and the food shortage (British army rations did not allow for any indulgence in luxuries, either), the lot of workers and management alike was far from being a happy one; it was a time well remembered by many of those veterans who still remain at the factory.

Although roof repairs and the general state of affairs had advanced somewhat, the hard winter of 1946-7 was to be even worse; temperatures dropped so low that lack of heating made it impossible to operate hydraulic equipment, including the big presses, and the factory had to shut down completely for some weeks.

Following a brief lull in January 1946, when only 83 vehicles were built, production steadily rose; in February the figure had reached 842 new Type 11 Beetles with normal, lower suspension, and by the end of

This view of the southern frontage gives some idea of the size of the factory at Wolfsburg. It was made up of four main buildings connected by passageways, with nineteen wings projecting at right angles from the main frontage. Each of these has its own dining hall capable of seating five hundred at once. In the foreground is the rear view of an air-cooled Tatra used as a staff car. Beetles and Kübelwagens were used to transport officers around the plant along the 1km perimeter road which ran the entire length of the main building. Piles of bomb debris can be seen by the road.

March the target of 1,000 cars a month had been reached, after which production continued at around the March figure.

To ensure quality of the product, and bearing in mind that the Beetle was being produced at that time solely for the British Occupation function, Hirst requested an inspection team from REME headquarters to carry out customers' acceptance inspection. Captain Charles Bryce, the factory's first British inspector, arrived in March 1946. The company, of course, already had an inspection department, but there were weak links, and in particular there was a shortage of equipment; a crack detector, for example, had to be borrowed from the British army. The Beetle being produced at that time left a lot to be desired and Bryce, at Hirst's invitation, had access to all stages of production.

Like the rest of the British staff, he worked through the German management. He had a busy time hunting out the initial bugs, like the aforementioned steering problems, plus a horde of other early production gremlins, such as oil-cooler faults traced to bad solder, bad con-rod forgings, poor castings for gear boxes and crankcases, weak shock-absorbers and extremely poor paint finish. Gradually, the quality-control function became better organised and standards improved, especially after an ex-Opel engineer had been appointed as chief engineer.

As the initial British requirement for Beetles was on the way to being satisfied, the Allied authorities in the other three Occupation zones asked for a share of the output. A quota system was accordingly operated at CCG headquarters. One batch of Beetles to leave what is now West Germany travelled east, to the Russian army in Eastern Germany; this consisted of about fifty cars finished in maroon, which were collected by Russian soldiers after some preliminary driving instruction at the factory. The French army took delivery of a much larger number about that time, 3,000 or so (finished in light grey) while many others went to the US army (in dark grey). Incidentally, in 1947-8, when Beetles became available to private individuals, American and British servicemen bought a considerable number, some of which found their way back to the States and to Britain before exports began to those countries. Smaller numbers were also allocated to agencies such as the Red Cross.

115

With allocations being made to the other Occupation zones, the Beetle even as early as 1946 was finding its way into every part of West Germany, and there was a growing need for after-sales service to keep the cars running. It is appropriate at this point to relate the measures taken by the factory to look after its customers, mainly the Allies at this juncture. These measures were described by Ivan Hirst who, like the rest of the British who were involved, must take some pride in having set the pace for Volkswagen's now legendary after-sales service. It should be remembered that the Volkswagenwerk had not yet operated as a normal car manufacturer and that their back-up for the German army's Kübelwagen seems to have been limited in scope. Hirst said:

> In the British army, repairs and maintenance had developed very rapidly. Largely because of the long sea routes to the Eighth Army in North Africa and to Burma, special emphasis had been placed on the availability of replacement parts, special tools, service manuals and parts catalogues. The British customers in 1945-6, and also ourselves at the factory, were very service-minded, but we found the German executives then at vw gave relatively little thought to after-sales service. They learnt a great deal from the British in this area of motor manufacturing.

The tasks to be dealt with in connection with after-sales service included writing the first driver's handbook, producing a parts catalogue with exploded diagrams modelled on British and American practice, developing and producing special tools for users' workshops, instituting technical-service bulletins, designing a defect-reporting system and eventually a reconditioned-assembly scheme (exchange engines, transmissions, and front axles). 'This last arrangement', Hirst commented, 'seemed to be unknown in Germany and after weeks of unsuccessful persuasion I had to give a formal order before anything was done in this respect.'

At a later stage, in 1948-9, the British army's REME scales branch had a team visiting Wolfsburg for a short time, to work out the scaling of vw spares. Scaling is a matter of deciding which and how many replacement parts and assemblies need to be held at different points in order to maintain a given number of vehicles in service. The German side benefited greatly from all such activities and as a result, had become 'service-minded' before the vw went in any quantities to the general public or for export. A classic example of the British staff's adherence to their after-sales policy came about in 1947, in connection with the first consignment of Beetles to the Dutch concessionaires, where Hirst recalls:

> Because of import licensing problems, they had ordered cars but no spares. Charles Radclyffe agreed with me that we had to make the point and the first cars stayed at Wolfsburg until the parts order came and was met. This action was not welcomed by vw management, or by the foreign conces- sionaires, but they learned the lesson.

The matter of the early dealerships in Germany was explained by Ivan Hirst, including the way in which they evolved:

> In 1946, most of the vws on the road were maintained by army or CCG workshops, but there were some, such as cars supplied to the coal industry in the Ruhr, to agencies like the Red Cross and to individuals on the British side, which did not have access to army or CCG repair facilities. The transport division of CCG, concerned with German transport matters including roads and garages, held a conference at Wolfsburg attended by ourselves (British and German staff at the factory), by British Mil Gov officers from all parts of the zone (many of whom in civilian life in the UK were in the motor trade), and by garage proprietors nominated by Military Government and by vw. This conference, the first vw dealer conference to be held, proved to be a very happy and successful affair and one which led directly to the vw distributor and dealer organisation within Germany.

Exports began in 1947, with the Pon brothers of Holland becoming the first foreign concessionaires. Ben and Wijnant Pon had taken a keen interest in the vw even before the war, but it was not until 8 August 1947 that a contract was signed making Pon's Automobile Company at Amersfoort the sole vw concessionaires for the Netherlands. Ben Pon's first approach to vw took place early in 1946, when he put on a Dutch army officer's uniform (the only way to enter Germany at that time was in uniform) and made his way to Wolfsburg. Owing to the fact that all available production at that time was against the Allied requirement, Pon's request to be appointed vw concessionaire for the Netherlands had to be left in abeyance. However, by early 1947 when the Allied requirement had been adequately met and there was an excess, firms such as Pon and a number of German agents were able to take deliveries.

With regard to exports, Ivan Hirst explained:

In 1945-6, the British zone of Germany was a heavy financial burden on the British taxpayer. The zones were more or less watertight divisions of Germany, and the British zone, which included the Ruhr basin, had a large population but relatively little farming; the bill for essential imports was high, and the German Reichsmark was worthless as an international currency. All of us in the CCG industry division were asked to promote exports. About this time the economic affairs of the British and US zones were merged, and in order to handle the finances of German imports and exports, a US/UK agency was set up, called 'Joint Export Import Agency'. Known in short as JEIA, this agency henceforth paid for the imports and received payments (in US dollars) for the exports.

Along with items like cameras, the VW was an obvious German product suitable for export. The car was shown at the first Hanover fair in 1947, and a flood of inquiries was received. The CCG board for the VW organisation held a joint meeting with JEIA at the factory and the board set up a direct link between JEIA and the German management, since it was they who would have to run the entire export operation at a later stage. Exports belonged to the future and we wished the German management to exercise full responsibility in this field.

We left the choice of concessionaires entirely to the German side. In those days there were no hotels or restaurants, so we arranged for our officers' mess to become a transit hotel. Until about mid-1948 the concessionaires and their representatives visiting the factory stayed there.

A total of 7,787 cars were produced in 1945-6, and all but a few (for the German authorities and essential services) were absorbed by the Allied requirement.

Apart from the normal saloon designated at that time as the Type 11 (later to be changed to Type 1), two special models were produced in the factory's experimental department, and were to be seen running around Wolfsburg. One was a cabriolet sometimes used by Hirst, and the other a two-seater roadster, used by Charles Radclyffe. The idea of putting a cabriolet into production seems to have been given some consideration but was ultimately put into the hands of outside firms,

Volkswagen Production 1945/46

1945	Type 11	21	28	51	83	93	Total
April							
May							
June		138					138
July		235					235
August	1	136	26	4			167
September		11	191	2		96	300
October	1	1	2	57	151	425	637
November	1			295	124		420
December	55	1		345		192	593
Total	58	522	219	703	275	713	2490
1946							
January	5			71		7	83
February	842	1		31			874
March	1001						1001
April	1002						1002
May	1052						1052
June	422						422
July	1000						1000
August	1353						1353
September	1000						1000
Total	7677	1		102		7	7787

WOLFSBURG MOTOR WORKS PRODUCTION TYPES, 1945-6: Type 11 - Beetle; 13 - Sliding Roof Beetle; 15 - Convertible Beetle; 21 - Kübelwagen; 25 - Kübelwagen Fire Tender; 27 - Kübelwagen Pick-Up; 28 - Kübelwagen Van; 51 - Beetle with Kübelwagen Chassis; 53 - Sliding Roof Beetle with Kübelwagen Chassis; 55 - Convertible with Kübelwagen Chassis; 81 - Beetle Pick-Up; 83 - Beetle Van, Reicespost Type; 91 - Open Trailer; 93 - Closed Trailer; 100 - Road Tractor (Short Beetle Pick-Up) who were supplied with standard saloon-body components and left to produce their own interpretation of the cabriolet.

The first of these coachbuilders was Karmann of Osnabrück, a well-established company, which was later to become vw's sole approved producer of the Beetle cabriolet. Representatives of Karmann spent two days at the factory in 1946, and whilst there held lengthy discussions with the German staff in the experimental department, where they had an opportunity of studying the factory's one-off jobs. This led to Karmann producing a number of prototypes, but there were problems with the lack of body rigidity, created by virtually slicing the top from a stock Beetle body. (The effect of cutting off the roof can be compared with the end result of cutting away one end of a tin can, which has the effect of weakening the structure as a whole.) The whole affair proved to be rather flimsy, creating excessive shake and poor handling characteristics. This problem was eventually solved by reinforcing the body

The one-off cabriolet. This was used as a pattern for the later Karmann cabriolet, put into production in 1949, which became the only official version.

120

Words fail when trying to describe this Type 100 Road Tractor, introduced in 1947 as a possible means of filling the commercial gap. Not surprisingly this bizarre model never went into production.

structure but it was to be a full three years before Karmann decided to put their cabriolet into production.

By drawing on old wartime stocks, the factory was able to build two more four-wheel drive Kommandeurwagen (Type 87) as an exercise aimed at demonstrating the Beetle's ruggedness. One of these was fitted with a front roller (an idea borrowed by Hirst from boyhood memories of Citroëns which crossed the Sahara Desert) and, aided by the extra traction afforded by the four-wheel drive, the Type 287, re-numbered from the old Type 87, created a certain amount of interest, particularly from the French, who wished to order one hundred Type 87s for forestry work in the Black Forest area. Unfortunately, the original dies used for the front-axle parts had been lost in Silesia along with those for

121

the KDF Wagen; consequently, these two were the only ones to see the light of day after the war (at least one of which has survived in private hands). When asked what these cars were like to drive, Hirst recalls that they were somewhat cumbersome, but the Kommandeurwagen had a fantastic all-terrain capability. With regard to the normal Beetle of those early days, he went on to say:

> With its general lack of refinement and its crash gearbox, hard springing, cable brakes and low power, the Beetle of 1945-6 bore only a family resemblance to its successors, but it provided economical and reliable transportation. Many drivers preferred its handling to that of the Beetles produced in the 'fifties. These versions had more power and softer suspension, but still retained the old swing-axle arrangement at the rear which could be treacherous on slippery bends.

Total production for 1947 stood at 8,987 cars. Today, this seems a very low figure but it has to be viewed against the backcloth of the time—production levels were still determined by the general shortage of steel and other materials such as rubber and glass, and the other major factor was the very poor financial climate with the almost worthless Reichsmark. It must also be remembered that the factory even as late as 1947 was still working primarily for the British and the other Occupation authorities. Though some cars were going to the German economy and for export, the continued existence of the plant was solely attributable to the four-year reserve placed upon it in mid-1945 for the Occupation requirements of the Allied powers.

It was, however, apparent to the British board that VW could have a viable future as a major car manufacturer, but no one could be certain, as the company was still ownerless, and the plant might go as reparations after the four-year reserve expired in 1949.

Nevertheless, considerable progress had been made on both the production and the management sides and, as Hirst recalls, 'The department heads (supplies, personnel, production and finance) appointed or confirmed in office by the British were settling down very well, but there was a need for a general manager since Brörmann had left on de-Nazification.' As a compromise with their Property Control colleagues, Radclyffe and Hirst agreed that the CCG board should appoint a worthy gentleman from banking circles in Berlin as custodian and general manager. Unfortunately, this individual turned out to have only limited understanding of an industrial undertaking and likewise another man he brought in as financial manager knew little about the motor industry or cars. After several unfortunate incidents, such as car production being stepped up above the schedule that was governed by the availability of materials and bought-out components, and the proposed first export shipment (to Holland) of cars without any spare-parts backup, Hirst recommended at a board meeting that they should continue to look for a good man from the industry, to be deputy general manager. This was agreed, and Hirst and Radclyffe undertook to look for suitable individuals. Initial inquiries met with no success until one day, as Ivan Hirst recalls:

> A British colleague in Hamburg told me about an ex-Opel man who was kicking his heels in that city. His name was Heinz Nordhoff. I asked him to Wolfsburg for a couple of days of factory visits and interviewing. His combination of earlier engineering training, experience of after-sales service matters, and his broad outlook, stemming no doubt from General Motors influence in Adam Opel, showed that he was our man. I 'phoned Charles Radclyffe in Minden, suggesting that Nordhoff should be offered the general manager job rather than the proposed post of deputy general manager. I sent him to see Radclyffe who later 'phoned me to say that he agreed with my assessment and suggestion. At its next meeting, the board formally agreed that the appointment of Generaldirektor should be offered to Nordhoff and that the custodian and general manager appointed earlier should retire. Nordhoff took up his appointment on 1st January 1948.

By late 1947, it was becoming clear that the company would have a future. The political climate was changing, and it was unanimously agreed that Nordhoff should be given a free rein, though he would still be responsible to the CCG board until it was replaced by some other form of supervisory board on eventual handover of the vw concern from British trusteeship.

Just prior to Nordhoff's arrival at the beginning of 1948, Hirst arranged for the outward signs of 'British control' to be made less obtrusive, eg, smaller British direction signs, more spaces for visitors' cars outside the factory offices and so on. Inside the company, the

British ceased to take direct action (no further direct instructions to middle management), except on matters directly connected with the Allied requirement of cars and parts. Hirst's main function changed.

As the only member of the CCG board remaining resident in Wolfsburg, I was to watch over the company's general development in case Nordhoff had not turned out to be the man we thought him to be. In the event, Nordhoff quickly proved himself to be the right man.

It is certainly true to say that the Volkswagen company today owes its existence to the British, for there is no doubt that had it not been for the British car requirement, the Wolfsburg factory would have gone as reparations, under the heading of 'surplus to post-war level of industry'. The gallant efforts of the small band of British officers during the initial setting-up period in 1945-6, and the benefits of British experience such as after-sales service, helped put VW well on the road to success.

Servicing has always been a strong Volkswagen point all over the world: here an undertray is being cleaned in the washing booth at the UK Plaistow works in the late fifties (*Havas*).

Ivan Hirst summed up this crucial period in the history of the Volkswagen as follows:

By the time Heinz Nordhoff arrived as Generaldirektor of the company, it was already well on the way to being a viable enterprise. The building repairs were well advanced, the press and body shops were functioning as originally intended, and the machining lines were laid out properly after bringing back the machines from the dispersal sites and factory cellars. Cars were going to the German economy and for export. After-sales service was well organised, with a good technical-service department (including service school, manuals, parts catalogues and service bulletins) and a good spare-parts organisation. The property control people had had a balance sheet drawn up—the first in the company's history, but costing was meaningless in those days. Moreover the situation was extraordinary; no interest had to be paid on the vast capital expenditure effected by the DAF in 1938-9 while, on the other hand, large sums were going to building repairs in 1946-8 and production levels were too low to be economic. Most of the credit, however, is due to the departmental heads appointed before Nordhoff's arrival and retained by him (production, supplies, personnel etc), and to the German workforce who had done a magnificent job in the hard times of 1945-7 and, I venture to add, the British connection, but it was not the work of any one man. It was the result of team work, German as well as British—just as the diverse Military Government interests had been brought together on the CCG Board for the Volkswagenwerk organisation. As for the British, by 1949 we had done our job, which was to get VW cars into production for Allied use in Germany, to help rebuild the West German economy, and to serve as trustees for an ownerless undertaking.

5

From Obscurity to World Fame:

Australia, New Zealand, Canada, South Africa and elsewhere

Heinz Nordhoff was born in Hildesheim in 1899. He started work as an apprentice with the Bavarian State Motor Works (BMW) in Munich. He later joined Opel, a subsidiary of the giant American company, General Motors. His first job with Opel involved him in the writing of service manuals, and in 1930 he was promoted to head of the service department. Nordhoff's insatiable appetite for work caused him to spend much of his spare time on the production line studying shop-floor methods and getting better acquainted with factory-floor personnel and the machinery that goes to make up the heart of any industrial concern.

During the course of his career with Opel he made several visits to the States, where he was able to study at first-hand the sales and production methods which had helped to turn the American motor industry into the largest and most successful operation of its kind. Like Porsche, he was deeply impressed by their up-to-date methods of mass production. He admired equally the informal relationships which existed between management and staff who worked together in a relaxed and cordial atmosphere.

He later became a member of Opel's board of directors, before moving to Berlin where, during the war period, he took charge of their giant truck factory at Brandenburg. At the end of the war, like millions of other Germans, he found himself amongst the unemployed, as the Brandenburg factory fell within the Russian sector of Berlin. He spent the next two years living a hand-to-mouth existence before receiving Major Hirst's invitation to come to Wolfsburg.

The irony of the decision to invite one of Opel's former senior men to take charge of the plant was well reflected in a speech made by Nordhoff in 1954. He was referring to those events which took place late in 1947, a time when vivid memories of pre-war Germany still lingered in the mind, when the threat of unfair competition from Hitler's people's car had cast a shadow across Germany's privately owned car industry, including his own company:

> In January 1948, when I took over the management of the vw factory, I regarded the Volkswagen with the utmost scepticism. It was tarred too much with the brush of political trickery, and the way it looked at that time was anything but a beauty.

However, Nordhoff's lifelong experience in the motor trade plus his level-headed approach made him the ideal candidate for the task that lay ahead. The hidden potential he could see in what was once Europe's largest automobile factory presented him with an irresistible challenge. His earlier reluctance and scepticism rapidly changed to inexhaustible enthusiasm for the Beetle.

For the first six months after taking up his new post, Nordhoff slept in a temporary flat near his office. With relentless drive and energy, working seven days a week, he set about his new job.

The 'Wolfsburg Motor Works' sign outside the main building was removed, with, as Major Hirst recalls, the full blessing of the British— a clear indication that the factory was once again under German management. The sign was replaced with one bearing the old name of 'Volkswagenwerk GmbH'.

Production at the time of Nordhoff's arrival amounted to just seven hundred cars a month, a figure which he knew would have to be dramatically increased if the factory was to have any kind of future as a commercially viable mass-production plant. Within a few weeks of his arrival he called together the whole of the workforce, to deliver what he later described as a stiff shock to all concerned. The message was blunt: the present rate of production was utterly miserable, and the four hundred hours it was taking to produce each car would have to be cut to one hundred hours. The initial reaction was that such an output was impossible.

127

Nordhoff was well aware of the hostile attitudes that could easily be evoked by the use of high-handed methods, so he chose to disregard the traditional conservative attitude of German management and instead concentrated on forming a closely integrated system, where management and staff cooperated in the task of raising the factory back to full production. He spent a considerable amount of time on the shop floor, explaining his intentions to individual members of staff, leaving them with a full appreciation of what he was trying to achieve. His honest approach earned him great respect, and the concentrated effort on the part of the workforce under their new German boss resulted in a marked increase in output. The combination of hard work, backed by the improvement in the availability of supplies, enabled production to be more than doubled over the previous year, with output for 1948 totalling 19,244 cars.

However, a considerable investment programme was required to raise production to profitable levels. The factory needed modern machinery, much of which would have to be purchased abroad in hard foreign currency. Under West Germany's new liberal economic policies such currency could only be earned by the exporting of finished goods. Nordhoff wasted no time in expanding the export programme first started by the British in 1947, when Ben Pon of Holland had become the first foreign buyers of the vw. In 1948 Volkswagens were exported to Belgium, Luxemburg and Switzerland, all of whose economies were free of currency restrictions. Denmark and Sweden followed suit in 1949. As there were as yet no shareholders in the vw company all profits from sale could be ploughed back. The home market was also rapidly expanding, with new outlets spreading right across the country, and by the end of 1951 there were 729 agencies in Federal Germany and West Berlin.

Volkswagen's reputation for after-sales service, which as will be recalled was first initiated by the British, owes much also to the methods laid down by Nordhoff in 1948. His principle, that a car is no better than its after-sales service, led to the establishment of a back-up organisation without equal. Under the rules laid down by the company, each dealer was required to carry a comprehensive stock of spares, totalling well in excess of 8,000 parts, ranging from the smallest items, such as contact-breaker points, to a complete car body. A fixed schedule of charges for servicing and repairs was laid down, and a sales manual giving detailed advice on selling techniques was made available to showroom staff.

When Nordhoff first took over the factory nobody had any idea how much a car cost to produce and the problem was aggravated by the diminished value of the Reichsmark. He therefore set up a proper accounting system, which operated throughout the plant, enabling the establishment of a final price based on proper costing procedures.

Housing was still a major problem in Germany and in order to attract skilled labour the company built four hundred new dwellings, consisting mostly of three-bedroomed flats in blocks three storeys high. This outlay formed part of the company's initial re-investment programme, along with the purchase of much modern heavy plant machinery, a considerable proportion of which was imported from the United States.

Nordhoff then turned his attention to the car itself. The vw being produced in 1948 was virtually identical to the pre-war version—a vehicle which left a lot to be desired. Nordhoff made this clear in 1954:

> It was badly sprung, badly painted, with mediocre brakes, a mediocre transmission, badly equipped and upholstered, noisy and hard riding, but above all, its engine had absolutely no durability; a pretty miserable duckling. But its designer, Professor Porsche, had worked something into it, which made this diamond very much worth our while to polish.

The revamping of the old Type 38 (the first pre-war designation) was to be total. Nordhoff called together his team of designers with a brief to modify every component, no matter how small. To achieve this, Porsche's old drawings were redrawn as many as ten times, until not one component exactly corresponded in size to the original. What eventually emerged was a car which was to be the hallmark of the Volkswagenwerk's post-war success. All this was achieved without altering the basic design, but merely improving on it; a task, incidentally, which took the designers a number of years to complete. Continuous modifications were made to the Beetle throughout the entire period of its manufacture. The Beetle's later reputation for reliability won it new friends in every country where

Nordhoff's 'miserable duckling'—badly painted and badly sprung it may have been, but it provided essential light transport at a time when other manufacturers were totally incapacitated.

it was sold. Even those who had previously viewed the car with a degree of anti-German sentiment began to appreciate its qualities, and the benefits of an efficient after-sales service.

Two events which took place in 1948 were to have a profound effect on the German economy, and were to mark a turning point in her destiny. The first was the introduction of the monetary reform laws, which came into effect on 20 June, aimed at ending the country's early post-war inflation and creating a stable economy. The old Reichsmark was withdrawn, and replaced by the Deutschmark, with an exchange rate of 1 Deutschmark to 10 Reichsmark. One of the initial effects of the new reforms was the virtual disappearance overnight of the savings of thousands of German citizens, but the benefits of a stable currency brought about a new stimulus to the German economy. The second important development of 1948 was the introduction of the American Marshall Plan, whereby millions of American dollars were pumped into the West German coffers. A new air of confidence began to emerge in place of the gloom of former years. Old stocks hoarded during the war period were brought out of hiding, small businesses came to life, traders began to trade, money began to circulate, and in industry there was a rapid rise in employment. Those who witnessed the transformation were over-awed by the incredible speed of the German recovery, which just seemed to happen overnight, turning the austerity and deprivation of early post-war Germany into a new era of prosperity from which she has never looked back.

vw's sales, in line with the rapidly improving economy, quickly accelerated on the home market, with the bulk of output for 1948 going to German dealers. Of the 19,244 cars produced only 4,464 went for export, and a small consignment went to the occupying forces.

One other incident which took place in 1948 under early post-war reparations was an offer from the Russians to take over the plant, simply by moving the border enough to place Wolfsburg within the Russian sector. This suggestion was flatly turned down by the British authorities.

To help match increasing demand, Nordhoff applied what he fondly referred to as 'vacuum pressure' to production: whilst large stocks of raw materials were kept inside the factory, he ensured the rapid disappearance of finished cars from outside; the psychological effect caused people to work harder, and so raise output, without the use of financial incentives.

On 6 September 1949 the British relinquished control of the factory, which, until the question of legal ownership could be firmly established, was placed under a trust run by the federal government and the state of Lower Saxony. Colonel Radclyffe, who had remained as chairman of the ccg board until 1949, died later that year. His number two, Major Ivan Hirst left the factory in the August (and later became a member of staff of the Allied Military Security Board in Germany, where he remained until 1955).

Certain accounts have suggested that Hirst was disappointed not to have had Nordhoff's job himself, which he described as nonsense. 'I was a British official doing what was required of me. And I have always taken the view that a German undertaking needs a German boss.' Later on, when he was offered a post as head of a German subsidiary of a British company, he refused for that very reason.

With the blessing of the German government, which encouraged Nordhoff to continue running the plant on a free-enterprise basis, the company's progress over the next few years was to mark an incredible achievement for both staff and management. The company was not responsible to shareholders and so was free to plough back the large profits from home and foreign sales into investment. The dream of the original designer, Porsche, of seeing his car rolling off the production line in vast numbers, as he had seen happening in America—a dream sadly shattered by the outbreak of war—was to be turned into a reality at the beginning of the 1950s, when, within an amazingly short space of time, Volkswagenwerk was transformed into a superbly efficient mass-production car plant, run on similar lines to its counterparts in the States. In fact, it was an achievement beyond even that dreamed by the car's original creator. The formula for this success was simple: to supply the world's car-hungry markets with a reasonably cheap and reliable vehicle.

A production total of 46,154 for 1949 did little to solve the problem of a six months' waiting list for delivery, and in order to meet demand Nordhoff ordered production to be doubled. This feat was all but achieved by the end of the following year, when the figure rose to 90,038.

Exports in 1949 accounted for only 7,128 of total production, with the bulk of sales going to the home market. The constant need to earn foreign currency to pay for new investment made export sales a priority, and in 1950 the export figures leapt to 29,387. This was achieved in various ways. When Nordhoff surveyed the market in 1948, he looked beyond Europe, and the United States with its insatiable appetite for motor vehicles must have provided an irresistible challenge.

The first attempt to break into the world's largest automobile market took place early in 1949 when on 17 January the Dutch importer and entrepreneur, Ben Pon, landed in New York accompanied by a 1948 Beetle. Acting as Nordhoff's emissary, Pon used the car as a demonstration model, hoping to raise interest among the motoring fraternity in America. But alas to no avail. The view of the American automobile pundits was unanimous: such a vehicle with its unorthodox appearance and design had no future on the American market. After selling the car at a knock-down price to a local dealer, a disappointed Ben Pon returned home. Upon receiving the news, Nordhoff decided to try again, only this time in person, reputedly armed with nothing more than a bunch of photographs. However the American motor trade was still not interested in the Wolfsburg wonder. Despite these early failures, two cars were shipped to the States later that year, via Holland, and in 1950 Max Hoffman of New York became the country's first importer of the Volkswagen.

An 'Export Model', available as a deluxe version in Germany, was introduced on 1 July 1949. Fitted with extra trim and equipment, it proved a popular choice on the home market as a slightly more expensive alternative to the standard model.

Another car to make its début that year was the two-door cabriolet from the well-established coachbuilders, Karmann of Osnabrück. They were officially appointed by vw to fit their hand-built, open-bodied version of the Beetle onto the vw chassis supplied by the Wolfsburg factory.

The demand for lightweight commercial vehicles was also seen as a lucrative market, which led to the introduction of the vw 'Transporters', a range based on a former model, the 'panel van'. Eight of the Transporters were put on display late in 1949, with production beginning at the Wolfsburg factory on 8 March 1950 with an initial output of ten vehicles a day.

The idea of a vw commercial vehicle had its antecedents as far back as 1946. In order to fill the gap in the factory's supply of fork-lift trucks (those in use at that time had been borrowed from the British army but they were in short supply), Ivan Hirst suggested a factory-built job. He drew a sketch of a vw chassis with controls moved back to a driver's seat over the engine, and a platform body in front of the driver. A

The first Export or De Luxe version, introduced in 1949 with additional trim and chrome hub caps, headlamp rims, bumpers and so on.

number of these vw-engined 'Flat Tops', as they appear to have been called, were built in the factory's experimental department, and remained in use for a number of years.

It was, as Ivan Hirst recalls, Ben Pon who came to him with the idea that these factory trucks would sell in Holland, where pedal tricycles with a platform body in front of the driver are commonplace even today, a means of conveyance clearly only suited to the flat country of Holland. Although nothing materialised, it did sow the seed of an idea. Experiments using the Beetle chassis for a number of prototypes proved unsuccessful, and so a new vehicle was designed completely from scratch. The chassis layout was similar to that used on large, forward-control commercial vehicles, with the driver right to the fore, and an air-cooled engine to the rear—instead of the more conventional position beneath the driver. This led to a few problems during its early development, but the outcome was a vehicle which, in its various forms, ranging from pickups, ambulances and fire tenders to minibuses, was to prove its popularity around the world, and has remained in production to the present day. The early models were produced in the Wolfsburg plant, but were later switched, on 8 March 1956, to a purpose-built factory at Hanover, some 50 miles (80km) from the town of Wolfsburg. On 1 November 1957, the Hanover plant also took over the production of all vw engines.

The rake-off from ever-increasing sales enabled the company to purchase a considerable amount of new machinery but, as profits grew, so did the demands from the workforce for increased pay. Nordhoff sensed the dangers of conceding to such demands and he made this clear to them in a speech in which he emphasised the need for restraint, and the utter folly of endangering the future of the plant, as well as their own, at a time when re-investment needed to take priority over personal gain.

The practice of keeping the workforce informed became vw policy, with periodic addresses from the Herr Direktor. There was also a company magazine which covered a wide range of topics both inside and outside the factory.

Mass production by way of automation, was the key factor in the company's quest for ever-increasing productivity, but Heinz Nordhoff never underestimated the importance of the human element in the success or failure of any industrial concern. Speaking on this subject in 1954 he said:

> The value of an industrial organisation is not made up of buildings and machines, not by capital and bank accounts, but by the spirit in which the thousands of people who work in it approach their work. It depends whether or not they have been successfully integrated into the common task or not. Machines and factory fittings can be bought from the factory catalogue—inexpensive ones for a few thousand marks and the dearest ones costing a million—and you can build factories as big and impressive as you like, as long as you have the money. But you cannot buy the spirit of an organisation for all the money in the world—you have to create it yourself.

It was the spirit of worker participation, brought about by the machinery of good labour relations, that enabled each and every employee to feel he or she was an integral part of the vw concern. The system of worker representation on the board was carried beyond the rules laid down under German law, and there was also a company profit-sharing scheme, giving each individual a vested interest in the future prosperity of the factory.

Production rose rapidly during the early 'fifties, with a total of 105,712 vehicles in 1951, with 35,742 sent for export. On the 5 October of that same year, the number of Beetles built since the war reached a quarter of a million. With a workforce which had grown from 10,000 in 1949 to 20,000 by 1953, Nordhoff began to step up the export drive even further. In 1954, the number of vehicles exported had risen to 108,839, and in 1955 there was a further jump to 177,657, with overall sales for that year of 329,853.

The ever-increasing influx of new factory personnel into the town created a serious housing shortage. To help solve the problem, vw formed their own housing corporation known as 'VW Wohnungsbau', and encouraged private developers to start building programmes. As the town expanded, so did the need for amenities; shops, schools, a five-hundred-bed hospital and a large open-air swimming pool were donated by the factory, and in addition two modern churches replaced the wooden huts which had previously served as places of worship for the Catholic and Protestant communities.

The miraculous post-war recovery of the Volkswagen factory was mirrored in the town of Wolfsburg which, by the mid-1950s, had formed itself into a thriving community buzzing with activity, in stark contrast to the small handful of buildings surrounded by a motley collection of wooden huts and muddy, unpaved streets, riddled with potholes, of only a few years previously. The irony was, though, that Wolfsburg had become exactly what had been intended before the war—the city of the Volkswagen. Unlike the state-financed 'people's car', however, planned as the only choice for its customers, the post-war vehicle had to sell on its own merits.

It is certainly true that the task of selling the Beetle during those early

136

post-war years was made easier by the dire shortage of cars in Europe at that time. But by 1954 the factory engineers had done their job in revamping the old pre-war car into a vehicle fit to take on the increasing opposition from other manufacturers, now fully recovered from the effects of wartime hostilities.

The practice of awarding drivers who had completed 100,000km (62,137 miles) free from major engine repairs, with a gold watch and dash plaque, was later dropped, due to the vast number of claims.

The Beetle was not entirely free from criticism and there were many who tried to persuade Nordhoff to change its shape, saying that he could not continue to sell the same old design year after year. But Nordhoff concentrated instead on improving the existing model and actually proclaimed that the car would be retained in that form for a long time to come.

The car, however, defied all its critics, and earned itself a reputation for reliability, versatility, and robustness the world over. This was a reflection on the high standards of workmanship and engineering in the factory, kept up by the elaborately detailed inspection system first initiated by the British and later perfected under Nordhoff. Each car was subjected to a detailed scrutiny throughout every stage of production and, finally, each finished vehicle was put through a rigorous series of tests before being allowed to leave the factory.

Less than ten years after the end of the war, Porsche's creation was beginning to sell around the world.

On 11 September 1952 the Beetle made its official début on Canadian soil, via Volkswagen Canada Ltd. On the 23 March 1953 Beetles started coming off the new assembly line at Sao Bernardo do Campo under the name of 'Volkswagen do Brazil'. The Brazilian company was established by German born Dr F. W. Schult-Wenk, who later became a naturalised citizen of Brazil. In the first four years of production the company used parts imported from Germany (knocked-down vehicles), after which the company progressed to entirely home-produced Beetles and Transporters. It gave a massive boost to the country of Brazil, which became

Latin America's largest manufacturer of automobiles, and also the largest German company abroad. In 1969, the company started producing its own air-cooled model, the 'Brasilia', a 1600-engined car developed from one of the German prototypes for the Latin American and Mexican market.

The first entry of Beetles into Australia took place in October 1953, when the Melbourne firm, Regent Motors (Holdings) Ltd, whose proprietor was Lionel Spencer, put their first Beetles on display in the company's Melbourne showrooms. They acted as distributors for Australia, but established an assembly line in 1954, when they signed a contract with a firm of coachbuilders (Martin and King) of Melbourne to assemble knocked-down Beetles and Transporters imported from Germany. Sales were slow at the beginning, but the car's reputation for ruggedness and durability was quickly established during its many entries in Australia's toughest motoring event, the Mobilgas, and round-Australia trials. It scored many victories, and a number of outright wins, which probably did more to sell the car to the Aussies than any normal promotional campaign could ever achieve.

The establishment of Volkswagen (Australasia) Pty of Melbourne (changed more recently to Motor Producers Ltd) took place on 6 December 1957. This was a joint venture, with 51 per cent of the shares owned by the Wolfsburg company. As it expanded, so did the number of Australian manufactured components, eventually culminating in a 100 per cent Australian Beetle. In 1964, Wolfsburg bought out the remaining shares and like the parent company, vw (Australasia) 'went public'. After a vast programme of expansion, the company followed Wolfsburg as an exporter of vws, with markets in New Zealand, Fiji, the Solomon Islands and New Guinea, to name but a few. Like many other countries the Beetle continued in Australia until 1978, when it was finally superseded by the new water-cooled range.

On 8 March 1956 Volkswagenwerk acquired the assets of the South African vw importers, Samad (South African Motor Assemblers and Distributors Ltd), run by the late Mel Brooks, who had started assembling knocked-down vws in August 1951, at an assembly plant at Uitenhage, initially formed for the purposes of assembling Studebakers.

The company also performed as an assembly line for Austin of England until 1956 when Austin built their own plant near Capetown. By this time vw production had already outstripped that of Studebaker by two to one. The demand for Beetles in South Africa created a massive waiting list, which during the late 'fifties justified a large investment programme, followed by an even bigger one in the mid-sixties, when the Uitenhage plant was expanded for the purposes of manufacturing wholly South African vws.

In 1954 Volkswagen were estimated to be the world's fourth largest auto manufacturer, only outstripped by the American giants. Its soaring sales were reflected in the company's annual turnover, which exceeded 1,000 million Deutschmark for the first time, and from 1954 onwards, a special annual bonus was paid to all employees.

Incentives to work were matched with incentives to buy, with a special price reduction, exclusive to the German market, of 150 Deutschmark off the saloon, and 500 Deutschmark off the cabriolet.

In 1955 Beetles were pouring off the production line at the rate of one thousand a day, which meant that more cars were then being produced in three months than were built in the first five years after the war.

On 8 August of that year a special celebration marked what must have been a proud moment for the Volkswagenwerk, when the millionth vehicle left the production line. Finished in gold, the car attracted a vast audience and international news media, and representatives from vw concerns right around the world came together to sing praises to the now truly ubiquitous Beetle. The celebration culminated with a national display in a specially erected stadium.

For services rendered to his country, Nordhoff was presented with Germany's highest civil honour, the grand cross, and in further recognition, he was made an honorary freeman of the town of Wolfsburg. In May 1955 he was made an honorary professor of Brunswick Technical University, having already been made a doctor of engineering at the same university in 1951.

1955 also saw the establishment of Volkswagen of America, at Englewood Cliffs, New Jersey, designed to promote the Beetle and raise its previously mediocre sales in the States, a move which was to have a far-reaching effect on vw sales in America.

By the mid-fifties vw's export drive was beginning to cause a degree of consternation from many of those countries to which it was exported. Like all German manufacturers, vw were able to take advantage of Chancellor Erhardt's special tax concessions on exported goods, much to the disadvantage of many of its foreign rivals. This led to the imposition of strict import controls in various countries to try to stem the tide of what was now the world's most popular small car.

Sports cars based on the vw chassis were far from new at that time, with a number of enterprising individuals and small firms having tried their hand at producing sporty-looking models since the war. On 14 July 1957 the company announced the arrival of the 'Karmann Gia', a stylish two-seater car, built by Karmann of Osnabrück, from a body designed by Gia of Turin. Like the cabriolet, the body was mounted on a Beetle chassis. Although rather more expensive than the Beetle, it proved to be a popular choice amongst those who wished to combine the virtues of the Beetle with the sporty appearance offered by the Gia. After receiving a couple of face lifts in the 1960s, the car remained in production until 1974.

Longevity was to become part of Beetle legend, with early examples still giving faithful service ten, fifteen and even twenty years after being built. Whilst mainly concerned with the business of producing new vehicles, the company never forgot its older models. In June 1958 they opened an engine-reconditioning plant at Kassel, works originally built before the war for the firm of Henschel, then partly rebuilt by the British and used as a store depot. It was entirely rebuilt for vw engines all over the world, sent back to Kassel for stripping, rebuilding, and then returned as good as new to help keep those early Beetles alive and running.

By the early 'sixties vw promotional literature boasted sales in 136 different countries, stretching right across western Europe, and on into Asia and Africa, North and South America, Australia and New Zealand —in fact, a truly international car.

The company's advertising literature, often lavishly illustrated, depicted the Beetle in every conceivable situation. Location shots from around the world pictured the Beetle traversing the white sands of Mexico, or the Badlands of Dakota, a mountain pass in Norway, or somewhere in central London.

Its ability to operate in extremes of climate was well demonstrated when, in 1963, an Australian Beetle, christened 'Antarctica I', spent twelve months at Australia's research base at Mawson on the South Pole. By the time it returned to Melbourne this polar Beetle had clocked up the best part of 1,500 miles (2,400km) in one of the most hostile environments the world can offer. Other than superficial damage, the car returned none the worse for wear and in good working order.

Shortly after its return from the South Pole Antarctica I became an entry in the tough Australian BP rally, covering a distance of some 2,000 miles (3,200km) in scorching hot conditions through the southeastern part of the country. The outcome was an amazing win for Antarctica I, a double feat much publicised by the Australian vw press who pointed out the irrefutable evidence that this was a car capable of holding its own where and whenever called on to do so.

The increasing demand both at home and abroad, required constant revision of production levels and massive new injections of capital for further modernisation and expansion, with American companies benefiting from the constant flood of orders for their highly sophisticated machinery, including large presses, cutters and milling machines. Automation progressively took over from previously heavily manned production lines, with row upon row of automatic machines capable of churning out components previously requiring a small army of machine operators and factory hands, now employed elsewhere in the ever-expanding production area. In 1958 Nordhoff ordered an enormous new investment programme which over a period of two years led to an outlay of 1,000 million Deutschmark.

In 1960, the company opened another factory at Brunswick for the manufacture of front-suspension components and tools.

Production figures for the late 'fifties and early 'sixties rose dramatically from 557,088 in 1958, of which 315,717 were exported, to

1,007,113 in 1961, of which 533,420 were exported. As the figures indicate, production had almost doubled within a space of three years, making vw the first European company ever to produce one million vehicles in a single year, with a workforce now totalling 43,000, turning out vehicles at the rate of four thousand a day.

On 22 August 1960 the question of legal ownership of the factory was finally settled, when Volkswagenwerk became a public corporation. Since the British had relinquished control of the plant in 1949, it had remained in the hands of a trusteeship under the auspices of the central government and the state of Lower Saxony. After a long legal wrangle between the two governments, lasting throughout the 'fifties, over rights of ownership, an agreement was finally reached which gave each side a 20 per cent interest in the company's assets, whilst the remaining 60 per cent was sold as shares to the public. vw employees were given first option of purchase, limited to nine shares plus one extra share as a gift from the company. A twenty-one-member supervisory board of directors was set up, which included two members from each of the two governments, the remainder being made up of bankers and representatives from the workforces of each of its plants elected by their respective workers' councils. On 16 January 1964 vw shares went on sale to the public, at a purchase price of 350DM with some reduction for people with old vw associations.

Another long-drawn-out battle was this time between vw and the KDF card holders. An organisation was formed on 7 October 1948 for the purposes of extracting compensation from the old vw GmbH established before the war. Legal proceedings had commenced as long ago as 8 May 1949 and were to drag on for twelve years, until finally on 18 October 1961 the company voluntarily agreed to give all those who had completed their original payments a choice of 100DM in cash or 600DM towards the cost of a new car, a gesture made in spite of the fact that an earlier court hearing had dismissed the claim against the company.

On 4 December 1961 vw celebrated the production of its five-millionth Beetle since the war. To mark the occasion, a special medallion, available in either gold or silver, was struck by the Bavarian State mint depicting Professor Nordhoff on one side and the Beetle on the other. The company also passed a new milestone in 1961 with an annual turnover which exceeded a million vehicles for the first time ever.

Another major step taken in that year was the introduction of the vw1500. The new car represented Wolfsburg's first departure from the Beetle, but changes were limited to body styling, and the new Type 3 car (the original Beetle being Type 1 and Transporters, Type 2) was little more than a Beetle in disguise, with a lower profile and with a more powerful 1500cc engine.

The Type 3 range (a station wagon, the 'Variant', joined the saloon in 1962) was thought by many to be a possible eventual replacement for the now sixteen-year-old Beetle, but the old car outlived all its other air-cooled relatives introduced during the 'sixties.

The tremendous increase in the size and output of the Wolfsburg factory during the late 'fifties and early 'sixties, created an industrial behemoth, with 10,000 machines spread over a production area of almost $10\frac{1}{2}$ million square feet. The demand for labour to man the ever-expanding factory created a major headache for the management. In an attempt to solve the problem, the factory started importing Italian labour, who were housed in a specially constructed Italian village on the outskirts of Wolfsburg. Another move to attract labour was the setting up of a factory-financed housing construction company, operated as a Volkswagenwerk subsidiary.

Production in the first half of the 'sixties rose at an astronomical rate and in 1965 output had reached an annual figure of one and a half million, with the ten-millionth Beetle making its début during September of that year.

In 1964 Beetles began rolling off two new production lines, firstly in Mexico (Volkswagen de Mexico) which began operations on 15 January, and later, on 1 December, another German plant was opened at the coastal-based town of Emden (selected for its port facilities). The Emden plant's function was to supply the export market, and in particular the company's biggest Beetle customer, the United States.

An indication of the size of the vw operation at that time can be judged by the total annual payroll which, for 1964, amounted to over 1,000 million Deutschmark.

vw's sales record had risen unabated ever since 1948, when Nordhoff first took over the plant, up until the mid 'sixties. But throughout this time, the company had relied almost entirely on the Beetle for its massive worldwide success. Alas, it was this reliance on a single model that was, ironically, to run the Volkswagenwerk into serious trouble during the late 'sixties, and almost brought the company to the point of bankruptcy in the early 'seventies.

The year 1966 saw the twelve-millionth Beetle, a triumph soon overshadowed by the recession which began to threaten West Germany. Measures taken by the West German government to put the brakes on the economy resulted in a slump in vw sales at home with consequent cutbacks by the company. In a desperate attempt to delay mass re-dundancies, Nordhoff instead chose what appeared to be the lesser of two evils, by putting the company's massive labour force on short-time working, which at least had the effect of spreading the jam, however thinly, amongst everyone.

Criticism of his policy of relying on a single model came from many quarters, including the finance minister, Herr Strauss. Nordhoff answered his critics by showing to the press details of no less than thirty-six different prototypes supplied by Porsche AG—who acted as design consultant to the Volkswagenwerk. But all the designs had one thing in common—they were air cooled—and in fact amounted to little more than Beetles in different guises.

Nordhoff had, however, already sensed the need to expand the range. Early in 1965 the company had bought half shares in Auto Union, now a subsidiary of Mercedes-Benz at Ingolstadt, which was also used as an assembly plant for Beetles. It was here, later in 1965, that vw introduced its first front-engined, water-cooled model, also the first post-war Auto Union model to take the now familiar marque of 'Audi'. The model, the 'Audi 70', gave the company an alternative to its air-cooled range without the high costs of development, as it had been developed by Mercedes as the DKW F102 earlier.

Up until 1965 vw had relied very much on Porsche for designs of new models, but steps were taken in that year to provide the company with its own research and development centre. This included Europe's most advanced wind tunnel capable of wind speeds of up to 90mph (145kph) and, during the late 'sixties, a new proving ground 15 miles (24km) north of Wolfsburg which included 60 miles (97km) of test measurements and speed tracks, plus an artificial hill, with a gradient of 5 to 32. The new test area, which covered 2,720 acres (1,128 hectares), was designed with the specific purpose of simulating every conceivable condition and hazard, including flooded sections and rough roads, to test to the full Wolfsburg's future generation of water-cooled cars which, by the time of completion of the test area in the early 'seventies, were already in the pipeline.

The late 'sixties and early 'seventies marked the zenith of Wolfsburg's air-cooled range. More powerful versions of the Beetle, first in 1965 with the 1300, followed in 1966 by the 1500, helped to extend the range, along with the 1600 TL introduced in 1965 as a successor to the old 1500—first introduced in 1961, and further complimented in 1968 with the introduction of a new model, the 411, which was to be the last entirely new air-cooled passenger car to come out of Wolfsburg.

The increasing gloom of recession led, early in 1967, to the introduction in Germany of a cheap, no frills, basic 1200 Beetle. Although popular with the cost-conscious public, it did little to offset the company's financial problems. The situation facing the company by late '67 was beginning to look increasingly grim. With flagging sales and dwindling profits on one side, and increasing criticism from government and private shareholders on the other, Professor Nordhoff, now in his sixty-eighth year, found himself becoming a public scapegoat. He hit back at the sniping, much of which came from the country's newly formed coalition government, by calling for tax concessions to help ease the burden of vehicle ownership.

By the beginning of 1968 things had begun to improve; Germany began to move away from its short period of recession, and sales began to pick up. But alas, too late for Heinz Nordhoff, whose health was beginning to give rise for concern to such a degree that plans for his retirement in 1969 had to be brought forward.

Karl Hahn had been picked out by Nordhoff to succeed him upon his retirement. After spending a period in the States where he had scored considerable success in promoting sales, Hahn had later returned to Wolfsburg as sales director but, as such, became a victim of the recession, and so fell from favour. In his place Dr Kurt Lotz, previously head of the Swiss-owned electrical giant, Brown Boveri, a man quite well known to Nordhoff, moved in on 1 June 1967 as Nordhoff's number two and deputy chairman of the board. The plan had been for Lotz to work alongside Nordhoff for about a year, before taking over, but Nordhoff's health had deteriorated so rapidly that Lotz found himself addressing the annual shareholders' meeting on 28 June. By this time Nordhoff had been admitted to a sanatorium in Switzerland, suffering from heart failure and Kurt Lotz was left in sole charge of the company. Despite his serious condition, Nordhoff recovered sufficiently to return to Wolfsburg in October but his recovery was to be short-lived for he collapsed after delivering a speech in Baden Baden and died on Good Friday in Wolfsburg's city hospital.

Numerous written accounts of Nordhoff's career as Volkswagenwerk's first and longest-running Herr General Direktor leave an overall impression of a super-energetic individual who, backed by the wealth of talent available from his senior members of staff and heads of department, many of whom were with the company right from the beginning and remained there until retirement, had raised the company from obscurity during those austere post-war days, into Europe's largest motoring manufacturer. When Nordhoff took over the factory in 1948 he did·undoubtedly face many problems which had to be overcome before the company could envisage any notable degree of commercial success, and this has tended to overshadow the invaluable contribution made by the British prior to Nordhoff's takeover which laid the foundation of vw's success. Nevertheless the post-war Beetle phenomenon would undoubtedly never have come about had it not been for Nordhoff. It was he who ordered the revamping of Porsche's old design and then used it to supply the world's markets with a cheap, versatile car. However, whether through pure fanaticism for air-cooled designs or blind faith in a car which just seemed to go on selling in ever-increasing numbers, it was Nordhoff's approach which led to the company placing so much reliance on one vehicle. Although he began to take steps to

146

diversify the range, these came too late. It was undoubtedly the heavy burden of the resulting criticism which helped to undermine his health during his final days with the company. Despite his critics, however, Nordhoff remained to the last a confirmed air-cooled man and, whatever else he may be remembered for, his name will always be inextricably linked with the Beetle. He continued his defence of the car as late as 8 January 1968, just before his death, when he said, whilst addressing a meeting of vw dealers at Wolfsburg:

> As an engineer who knows many cars—and quite apart from the fact that I am a Volkswagen man—I would always rate the good old Beetle as one of the happiest combinations amongst the automobiles of the world.
>
> You will understand me when I say very emphatically that the star of the Beetle is still shining with undiminished brightness and you see for yourselves every day what vitality there is hidden in this car which has been pronounced dead more often than all these designs of which hardly a memory remains. I am absolutely sure that our Beetle will be produced for a very long time to come.

On 29 October 1968 the company's fifteen-millionth Beetle made its début. The car was still being produced at the rate of almost five thousand a day throughout the world, with the lion's share of the market going to the United States, who imported 423,008 Beetles during 1968. But this was sadly to mark the climax in Beetle sales to the States, for after this sales went into a steady decline. Following close in the footsteps of the Beetle, sales of vws Type 2 and Type 3, after reaching their peak in the States in 1970, began to drop off rapidly.

In 1969 the company acquired the assets of NSU, which they merged with Audi to form a new company called Audi NSU Auto Union AG, a move which gave them a new model, the 'K70', first developed by NSU at their Neckarsulm factory, and produced at a new plant at Salzgitter.

vw added yet another string to their bow in 1969 when they joined forces with Porsche of Stuttgart to form a jointly owned company called vw Porsche, with the specific purpose of producing sports cars. This led to the introduction of the vw Porsche 914, a rear-air-cooled-engine sports model. It was abandoned in 1974 when Porsche introduced their new '2 plus 2' sports car.

147

The 'vw 181', a multi-purpose, jeep-like vehicle made its début in the autumn of 1969. Reminiscent in appearance to the old wartime Kübelwagen and powered by a 1.6-litre, horizontally opposed, air-cooled engine, this robust model called the 'Thing' in the USA was a useful basic cross-country type of vehicle.

At the beginning of the 'seventies the company were producing a mixed range of air-cooled and water-cooled models in its eight German factories. (The eighth, at Salzgitter, began production in the autumn with the new vw K70.) The labour force, including its overseas subsidiaries, totalled 155,000, 54,000 of whom were employed at the Wolfsburg plant.

Despite all its attempts to diversify and broaden its range, vw's share of the home market in 1971 stood at only 22 per cent. Even worse was the drop-off in sales to its biggest customer, the USA, a situation brought about in part by the revaluation of the German Mark, and also by the rising cost of production. There was a reduction in Beetle sales alone totalling 50,000 in just twelve months. In a bid to speed up development of an entirely new range of cars, planned for introduction in 1975, the company began pouring vast sums of money into its development programme, just at a time when profits had slumped to an all-time low. Criticism of company policy by shareholders drove Lotz into resigning. He was replaced by Rudolph Leiding, an old vw man, who had joined Volkswagenwerk in 1945 as an engineer.

Leiding cut back on the existing investment programme, which involved the scrapping of a mid-engined car designed by Porsche, and instead concentrated on producing the new range of Audi cars. This led to the introduction of the 'Audi 80' in July 1972. This was later marketed in June 1973 under the vw label as the 'Passat'.

The new cars proved an immediate success and the company's future began to look a little rosier again. More staff were taken on and by 1973 the workforce stood at 161,000. By this time there were 2,500 vw dealers throughout West Germany and a grand total of 10,000 service centres throughout the world, with vws selling in 140 different countries.

The 1971 Beetle range saw the deletion of the 1500 to make way for the new 1302, with new front suspension and double-jointed rear axle, a car easily distinguishable by its bulbous bonnet.

148

Available in two engine sizes—1300 (the 1302) or 1600cc (the 1302S), it remained in production until 1972 when it was replaced by the 1303, a Beetle designed specifically to meet American regulations. Although similar in many ways to the 1302, the new model also available with either 1300 or 1600 engines, had a curved windscreen and reshaped wings, plus larger rear lights. Like its predecessor, the 1302, the 1303 remained in production for only two years, being phased out in 1975, although it continued to be produced by Karmann as a cabriolet.

1974 also saw the last of the remaining air-cooled passenger cars, namely the vw412, the 411's successor. The Beetle was left once again, after thirteen years, as the only air-cooled car, now amidst an array of water-cooled models.

Since 1945 the invincible bug has celebrated many happy occasions, but its greatest milestone was passed on 17 February 1972 when the 15,007,034th Beetle came off the production line, beating the record previously held by the Ford Model T. To mark the occasion, the company produced a large batch of World Champion' Beetles decorated with a plaque, and finished in metallic paint.

The improvement in the company's fortunes in the early 'seventies was to be cut short by the effects of the sharp rise in oil prices during the autumn of 1973 for these created a recession in the world's car markets. The effects of this on the Volkswagenwerk made the recession of 1967 seem minimal by comparison, and it was to place the future of the company in real jeopardy. During the following twelve months 11,000 members of the workforce were made redundant and widespread short-time working and temporary lay-offs were introduced.

The continuing decline of vw sales in America played a major part in the grim situation facing the company, with total sales to the usa dropping from 476,295 in 1973 to 334,515 in 1974, a loss of 142,000 vehicles in just one year. Overall export figures dropped from 1,224,809 to 976,105 over the same period. The decline in exports to the United States was certainly in part due to the continuing devaluation of the dollar, but also to criticisms levelled against the Beetle by a well-known American environmentalist which did little to enhance the car's image. The Beetle accounted for a large proportion of the losses incurred over

149

this period. The continual decline in the value of the American dollar, plus increased production costs, partly due to higher wages, sent the price of the Beetle rocketing in the States, as was clearly evident from suggested retail prices, which rose from $2,000 in 1972, to $2,625 just one year later. The cost of the Beetle had risen more in those twelve months than in the previous eighteen years.

The home market fared little better, with a sales drop of 20 per cent over the same period and by the end of 1974 company losses over the previous eighteen months had reached a staggering 800 million marks. A considerable proportion of the blame for these alarming figures was attributable to the new model programme which, despite previously mentioned cutbacks, had gobbled up a mind-boggling $2\frac{1}{2}$ billion marks, leaving the company with an increasingly large debt.

On 1 July at exactly 11.19am the last Beetle left the production line at Wolfsburg. Production of the Beetle continued at both Emden and Hanover and there was an assembly line in Brussels. However, Beetle body pressings and a variety of other components were still being manufactured at the Wolfsburg plant. Its sales still accounted for 50 per cent of the company's total output, and world production at that time stood at 1,700 Beetles a day.

The Beetle's place at Wolfsburg was taken by the 'Golf', one of vw's new family cars with front, transverse, water-cooled engines, introduced to the press in June 1974, just two months after its big brother, the 'Schirroco', built by Karmann of Osnabrück in place of the Karmann Gia. The smallest model in the new range, the 'Audi 50', arrived in September, followed in June 1975 by the vw version of the 'Polo'.

However, oil prices and the even higher production costs sent the company further into the red. There was a steep drop in vw's share of the European market and a continuing fall in sales to the States. This placed an intolerable burden on Leiding who, in a desperate attempt to revive the company's fortunes, put forward plans for an American-based assembly plant to reduce costs and boost its new range in what

Forty years of Volkswagen—the Beetle standing next to the VW Golf, currently the most successful vehicle being produced by the company.

had always been VW's biggest market. But Leiding found himself up against a stone wall created by the refusal of both government and unions—the latter for fear of mass unemployment—to even consider such a proposal.

By the close of 1974 the company's total losses amounted to over 800 million Marks, with exports the lowest for seven years. Trapped between government and union officials on one side, and diminishing sales on the other, Leiding eventually resigned on 10 January 1975 on the grounds of ill health.

Rudolph Leiding's resignation was in many ways tragic for, although he had only spent just over three years at VW, he had managed despite crippling odds to achieve precisely what was needed to set the company back on the right road. That is, he rationalised its new model programme, in particular the new Audi range, and this has since given the company a completely independent range of vehicles. At the time of Leiding's resignation VW had established a range of models sufficiently advanced to take them well into the 'eighties. They arrived only just in time before diminishing Beetle sales were set to drag the company into possible liquidation.

Despite the steady decline in exports from Germany, the Beetle, now only available as a standard or de-luxe model of the 1200cc-engined car, remained in production throughout 1976 and 1977, having triumphantly passed the eighteen-million mark on 4 October 1974. World production remained at around $2\frac{1}{2}$ thousand a day.

By 1977 VW's new generation of cars were well established and the company, having recovered from the setbacks of the early 'seventies, was enjoying renewed prosperity.

An upturn in sales on the American market reflected the popularity of the new water-cooled models. The hard lessons of the past had taught the company not to place too much reliance on the market of just one country, to concentrate more on the combined European market and to under-produce rather than the reverse.

The new VWs were greeted initially with a degree of scepticism from Beetle enthusiasts. After all, the Beetle had been around for a very long time, well before some of its younger owners had been born—'time enough to iron out the bugs', to quote one of the slogans used to promote the company's oldest creation. But history, as on many previous occasions, was to prove capable of repetition, and just as those who had been sceptical of the Beetle had come to appreciate its qualities so the generation of today have come to hold the Beetle's successors in high esteem.

Individual personality has always helped the Beetle to compete with the increasing number of compact models and although VW's newer models are worlds apart from it in design, one ingredient inextricably links both old and new, and that is quality. This quality will also enable the many Beetles throughout the world to remain in use for many years to come.

152

The cessation of Beetle production in Europe took place on 19 January 1978, when the last car came off the remaining production line at Emden, marking almost thirty-three years of continuous production in Germany. Although no longer produced in the German factories, the Beetle is still being built in Mexico and Brazil. Germany has since reversed its role as Beetle exporter to that of importer, with Mexican-built 1200 Beetles available exclusively to the German and Austrian markets.

One question often asked is whether the Beetle will ever make a comeback in those countries where it is no longer available. This is unlikely, if only because of the resounding success of Wolfsburg's new

The 1977 (1200L) model, the last of the line. Countless modifications had been carried out over the years but in outward appearance the unforgettable Beetle shape has been retained. Details of the principal modifications in the models over the post-war years are given in Appendix 2.

153

cars. But there is consolation in the fact that Beetles seem to outlast most other makes and that vw—as owners of older vehicles are particularly aware—hardly ever turns its back on the requirements of its customers when they need spare parts.

First conceived by Professor Porsche almost half a century ago, and then developed as a means of providing the world's most notorious dictator with a giant-sized piece of motorised political propaganda, the KDF, after failing to reach mass production, disappeared beneath the ashes of World War II. Save for the dire needs of the occupational forces it would probably have remained buried forever but, with little or no means of private transport at their disposal, the British decided to resurrect it along with the giant car factory. Through one man's vision the car became the most popular in the world, and a means of transport for people as diverse in nationality, class and creed as the number of roles which Porsche's creation has fulfilled during its thirty-four years of production. It is a vehicle which has become just what its creator wanted it to be—a Volkswagen or people's car.

6

The Beetle in Britain

In the winter of 1946 a lone Beetle accompanied by an experimental Hillman Minx took to the roads of Warwickshire. The route selected, which included the testing gradients of Friz Hill and Edge Hill, was part of a rigorous road test on the performance of the Beetle. vw cars were virtually unknown in Britain although a Kübelwagen had been captured in 1943, The Minx was included for comparative purposes. This particular vw, one of the earliest to leave the production line at Wolfsburg after the war, was certainly one of the first Beetles to enter Britain. The results of the road test and a meticulously detailed analysis covering every aspect of the car from engine layout to a detailed breakdown of the body structure were later published and made available through His Majesty's Stationery Office.

Although the report was favourable in parts, the car also came in for much criticism. Complaints of excessive engine noise, lack of power and poor braking, to name but a few, did little to enhance the car's image. The report concluded with a brief summary that read as follows:

> The car is painted entirely in army green, and this is an exceedingly poor finish. No adequate measures seem to have been taken either for cleaning or de-greasing the pressings before priming, or any steps taken for rust-proofing, with the result that the paintwork is peeling away from the metal. It is our considered opinion that from the body-engineering point of view the design of this vehicle is exceptionally good, and shows a great advance on previous constructional methods, but workmanship and general finish leave much to be desired and could be improved.

Although the vw compared favourably with the Minx on a number of aspects, by and large it was left looking a little jaded.

In those austere post-war days, with the natural suspicions which would undoubtedly plague such an unorthodox vehicle, importing the vw for the British market must have seemed a risky venture for anyone, even the most optimistic. Such optimism was, however, to be found in two motor-trade entrepreneurs, one living in Surrey and the other in Dublin. Both of them, by 1953 when the first concessionaireship for the UK was established, were already well-experienced members of the Volkswagen trade.

First on the scene was the late John Colborne-Baber who had been established for many years in his own motor-trade business on the Portsmouth Road at Ripley in Surrey. After the war he set about building up the business which, by 1945, already employed a number of mechanics. John Baber's first introduction to the Beetle took place in 1948, when a Swedish gentleman who had just returned from Germany arrived on the forecourt with a 1947 Beetle. As the vw was entirely unknown in Britain at that time, Baber made a number of inquiries within the motor trade, but nobody knew anything about the car, or had any idea of its value. A sale however was effected, and the Beetle taken in part exchange against a Buick for the princely sum of £150.

John Baber's early impressions of the Beetle can best be summed up in his own words: 'After running the car for about ten days, I decided that this vehicle was streets ahead of anything I'd ever driven in the small-car class.' By this time he had already made up his mind to specialise in the vw, feeling that this was a car which would sell around the world. This first Beetle, more affectionately known by its registration number, JLT 420, was sold to a Mr Andrew Leech, and then later repurchased in exchange for another second-hand Beetle.

The only vws entering Britain at that time were those brought back by the CCG people on their return to Britain. John Baber therefore placed advertisements in the *Motor* and *Autocar* magazines, publicising the fact that Colborne Garage were to specialise in the vw. He offered to purchase both cars and spare parts—which were supplied in special packs to owners taking their cars outside Germany. As an experienced motor trader, John Baber was fully aware of the problems to be faced when selling a completely new car like the Beetle in Britain, particularly without any after-sales-service facilities, hence his efforts to establish

The Colborne Garage forecourt in the late 'forties, with JLT 420 and other ex-CCG cars.

a spare-parts depot, whose initial stocks were made up from the spare CCG parts packs.

Although deeply impressed by the Beetle's performance, which John Baber described as a little saloon which drove like a sports car and utterly superior to any of its British competitors at that time, he did feel the need for some improvement to both the paintwork and interior upholstery. Consequently, the CCG cars purchased by Colborne Garage were re-sprayed, and the cheap hopsack seating re-upholstered in leather—due to a tax anomaly, leather actually worked out cheaper than rexine, giving the customer a choice of colours with matching interior. By 1951, these customised Beetles were selling for £410 and, if modified to right-hand drive, for £425.

Spare parts, however, became in short supply. Some small items such as oil seals found their way to Ripley by back-door methods and others were manufactured locally. This was still, nevertheless, totally inadequate to meet the needs of the small band of Beetle owners. Many of these made regular trips to Ripley to have their cars serviced, coming from all over the south of England and even, in one case, all the way from Swansea.

John Baber's next move was a trip to Wolfsburg in JLT 420, accompanied by Colonel McEvoy, the REME officer who first spotted the potential of building VWs as light transport in 1945, now back in England as a civilian. The purpose of this visit was to obtain a franchise to import spare parts through a small private company called the Baltic Supply Co. founded by McEvoy just prior to the war, when he imported Steyr cars from Austria. Under prevailing import regulations it appears that only those firms who had been importing before the war could be granted import licences which, of course, included McEvoy's company.

Pending an import licence from the Board of Trade, McEvoy was granted a franchise to import spare parts, with John Baber acting as a retail outlet. After pointing out the unfairness of a £120 purchase tax and import duty imposed on the CCG cars—for which there were no service facilities—John Baber persuaded a sympathetic Board of Trade to grant the necessary import licence.

In 1952 John Baber again travelled to Wolfsburg where he met Heinz Nordhoff, who granted him a franchise to sell new cars. The import licence, however, restricted John Baber to supplying only foreign visitors to the UK, in this case US forces personnel stationed at Manston air-force base in Kent. With Britain's need to earn American dollars, John Baber had convinced the Board of Trade of the Beetle's good qualities and its sales potential.

It was at about this time that John Baber acquired the first British concessionaireship for Porsche cars, which he later sold to the present owners. The first Porsche to arrive in Britain, during the first quarter of 1953, travelled from Stuttgart via the Hook of Holland aboard the ill-fated British Railway ship 'Duke of York' which, after being struck by the American freighter 'Haiti Victory', lost its bow section. The stern section, however, was towed into Harwich harbour with the Porsche still on board.

Although only about twenty new cars were sold prior to 1953, John Baber recalled that something in the region of one hundred of their refurbished cars were sold in the period 1948-52. It was John Baber's unending enthusiasm for the Beetle which led to him founding the Volkswagen Owners Club of Great Britain, even before new Beetles became available to the British public. Baber acted as the first president and funds raised by the club from its various functions were given to charity. The club still enjoys considerable popularity today.

John Baber also founded Britain's oldest and longest-running vw magazine, *Beetling*, initially a newsletter for the club. This later developed into a magazine and still enjoys considerable popularity under its present editor, Paul Harris. It contains a host of information on all aspects of vw ownership, from technical information to the latest vw news, as well as numerous articles on vw history. A question which often appears concerns the name 'Beetle'. This nickname, which was

When the 200,000th Volkswagen was exported to the UK in the mid-sixties it was decorated with flowers at Wolfsburg, in the German tradition.

159

later officially adopted by Wolfsburg, appears to be almost as old as the car itself. Indeed, Gordon Wilkins in his vw article in *Motor* as early as 8 May 1946 used the name and so, undoubtedly, have a great many other people when searching for an apt description for Porsche's creation.

There can be no doubt, however, that John Baber played a major part in publicising the name. Whenever he was spotted at the wheel of JLT by local children they would all shout, 'Here comes Baber in his Beetle,' and this caused him to adopt the name and use it for the title of his newsletter.

Whilst John Baber was selling his customised Beetles, Stephen O'Flaherty, founder of a company called Motor Distributors Ltd of Shelbourne Road, Dublin, having acquired the vw franchise for the Irish Republic, had the honour in 1950 of seeing his company build the first Beetle outside Germany, on a new assembly line using knocked-down cars imported from Germany. From 1950-77 the company produced a total of 72,000 Beetles.

Stephen O'Flaherty had joined the motor trade in the early 'thirties when he worked for Henry Ford and Co in Cork. After the war he launched out on his own with the assembly of twenty Adler cars purchased at a customs auction. He later extended his operations to cover the importation of a wide range of vehicles, including Porsche cars, jeeps, trucks and even electric vans. In 1953, when import restrictions in Britain were lifted to allow some sale of foreign cars, both Stephen O'Flaherty and John Baber set their sights on the concession-aireship for the UK.

This prize eventually went to Stephen O'Flaherty but, in view of his services to vw, John Baber received an eight-county distributorship, which was later reduced to a more manageable size to include just Surrey and Kent.

Under the able proprietorship of John Baber's son, Peter, Colborne Garage was completely rebuilt in 1970 when the family purchased a second garage at Peasmarsh on the outskirts of Guildford. Forty years later, Colbourne Garage continues to enjoy success, and JLT 420 is still a member of the family and acts as a permanent reminder of the car upon which the Baber family built its earlier success. Today the Colborne forecourt and showrooms display the wide range of vehicles available from Volkswagen and its sister company Audi, but the Beetle is still lovingly remembered by Peter Baber and his publicity agent, Francis Clarke. (It was Francis Clarke who was able to provide an account of John Baber's career, invaluable in compiling this interesting but rather forgotten story of a true vw pioneer, with a tape recording of a discussion between the two men shortly before John Baber's death in the early 'seventies.)

In order to raise capital for what must have proved to be a more expensive venture than was first envisaged, O'Flaherty, as head of the newly formed Volkswagen import company, trading under the name of vw Motors, invited K. J. Dear and Stanley Grundy to join him as partners in his new venture.

In June 1953 the company moved into its first premises at Inego Place, Bedford St, London. K. J. Dear was made managing director, with a number of other new members of staff being taken on to the payroll. The accommodation at Inego Place, located within the premises of O'Flaherty's solicitors, proved immediately inadequate, and in July new premises were taken above the Lotus showrooms in Regent St, London.

One of the first tasks undertaken at the new headquarters was the formation of a two-tier system of distributors and dealers. Press notices brought forth a flood of applicants only too willing to sign up with the new company. Amongst the applicants who applied were many who had been left stranded with the collapse of the Jowett company of Bradford, Yorkshire; others were desperate to boost their stocks as there was a great shortage of cars in Britain at that time. (This was due to a priority given to the export market—which applied to all goods manufactured in Britain then.) With very little time available and many of the large and well-established dealers unable to consider joining vw for fear of losing their existing franchises, it was very much a case of selection at random rather than choice, a situation that created many problems for vw in the years to follow.

Six months had elapsed since the formation of vw Motors and they still lacked any facilities for handling vehicles and spares, let alone a

161

showroom for display purposes. To add to the difficulties, a telephone call was received from Wolfsburg inquiring how many vehicles the company wished to order. Taking the plunge, O'Flaherty ordered two hundred cars—a decision that utterly astonished his staff. With no means of assessing demand and no facilities to handle the vehicles on arrival, the action could have been foolhardy, but the arrival of the first batch of twenty cars was met with understandable jubilation after many months of hard work and careful planning, for it gave a new credibility to the company, and the little cars, finished in gleaming black paintwork, must have proved a welcome tonic.

Meanwhile, new premises had been located in St James St, London, complete with showroom. To avoid the added expense of storage, the cars were delivered to the dealers as quickly as possible, and each distributor received a minimum of four cars plus £250 worth of spares. J. J. Graydon, who later replaced K. J. Dear as managing director and remained with the company until retirement in 1968, took charge of the sales side.

The company had its fair share of problems in those early days. Vandalism, probably the result of anti-German feeling, proved to be a major headache, with no less than 75 per cent of all vehicles suffering damage of some description. The problem arose whilst the cars were parked at High Meads, a collection centre where the cars were taken after they were docked at Harwich. The situation became so alarming that after discussing the matter with Nordhoff, the company decided to have just another three months' trial before abandoning imports altogether. Happily, as J. J. Graydon recalls, the vandalism suddenly ceased. To help eliminate this and other problems, a ship was chartered to deliver the cars to London, where dealers would collect and drive them to their final destination. (There were no transporters for the home market until 1955.)

The housing of spare parts was another major problem and, for a brief period in 1953, J. J. Graydon found himself sharing basement accommodation at St James St not only with the spare parts, but with a number of cars also. Another venue was sought to house the ever-increasing stocks. With the help of Dick Berryman, the wartime wing commander who served at Wolfsburg in 1946 and was now working as general manager for Moon's garage near Claridge's Hotel in London, a spare-parts depot was established in the basement at Moons, which served the company until the following year when a new depot comprising some 50,000 sq ft (4,650 sq m) of old railway sheds was established at Plaistow.

At the end of 1953 a total of 945 cars had been sold, with a first-year loss of £4,024, figures that could not have inspired much optimism amongst sales staff, and which showed the extent of the difficulties that would have to be overcome before any success could be achieved. The fight to improve sales proved to be formidable, requiring great determination on the part of the company.

Britain by tradition had always been a nation of small-car producers; the Beetle, of course, fitted very much into this category, consequently bringing it into direct competition with British cars, and the loyalties of the British motoring public remained firmly on the side of the British manufacturers. Added to this was the anti-German sentiment that still persisted. All in all it requires little imagination to appreciate what VW were up against.

The company's battle for survival, let alone an increase in their share of the market, required superhuman effort on the part of the staff. Much of the credit for the Beetle's success in Britain can be attributed to the gallant work of the VW men who worked for the company in those early years. In 1954 sales increased three fold to a total of 3,260 and by 1957 had increased to 5,000 per annum, which was encouraging. Although there was no reason for celebration yet, the car was at least holding its own.

Sales were also being restricted by the import licensing system, which remained in force until 1958. Under the system of import quotas implemented by the Board of Trade, an overall annual quota of imported vehicles was worked out, with each importer being granted a proportionate amount of the total national allowance. The problem with this system was that it did not take into account the individual needs of the companies. Whereas some companies like VW were screaming out for increased allocations, others failed to take up their full options. In order to try to solve the problem, J. J. Graydon ascertained from the company's competitors the individual requirements of each concessionaire. He then went to the Board of Trade where, with the consent of his competitors, he presented his findings, and succeeded in taking up the surplus allocations over and above the other foreign car traders' requirements.

Having sorted out their problems with the Board of Trade, vw Motors were faced with a crisis which threatened to halt their entire operation. In line with factory policy, the company had loaded its distributors and dealers with quantities of spare parts and, as J. J. Graydon remembers:

> We were informed by the factory that, owing to world demand, they were unable to supply any more cars. This could have put us out of business, so I went to Wolfsburg and put the situation to Heinz Nordhoff. He solved the problem by getting the factory staff to work Saturdays to supply the UK.

In 1957 it became clear that if the company was really to expand much more capital would be required, and so vw Motors became part of the Thomas Tilling group of companies with the late Lord Brabazon as president.

By 1961 vw could boast well in excess of thirty thousand Beetles on British roads. Although this was a limited success, at least the cars had achieved some degree of acceptance by the British motoring public.

One of the factors which helped to sustain sales throughout this difficult period was the tremendous enthusiasm displayed by vw owners. The Beetle quickly established a reputation for reliability among new owners and the growing vw brigade helped to dispel suspicions about the strange little rear-engined car.

Nordhoff's custom of awarding drivers who attained 100,000 miles (160,930km) without major overhaul spread to Britain where the prize was a diamond pin, presented by J. J. Graydon. He still remembers with great pride the ever-increasing number of Beetle owners who qualified for this novel award.

Many members of the motor-repair trade had little knowledge of the vw beyond basic servicing and their repair work was often much to the detriment of the car. In one case a member of the author's family entrusted his car to a local garage, which after stripping the engine down almost to the last nut and bolt, was unable to carry out the task of reassembly. The car, complete with dismantled engine, had to be transported some 30 miles to the nearest vw agent, much to the embarrassment of all concerned.

The beginning of the 1960s marked the turning point in the fortunes of the company. Gone were the dark years of the early post-war period which had lingered on through the 'fifties. Britain was at the start of a new era which was to bring prosperity and an exciting, new chapter for the Beetle in Britain. Memories of wartime hostilities which had done so much to hinder progress for the company in the 1950s had begun to fade. Sales began to accelerate. In 1964, the company celebrated its 100,000th vw to enter Britain since 1953.

A further landmark that year was the opening of a £1 million distribution centre at Ramsgate occupying some $23\frac{1}{2}$ acres ($9\frac{1}{2}$ hectares) of land. Cars and spares were landed at two special quays in Ramsgate harbour, transported one mile to the distribution centre, and then passed through a de-waxing and preparation plant, which opened in 1962 and was capable of handling a hundred cars per day.

By 1965 sales had reached an average of 28,000 per annum, increasing to 33,000 per annum in 1967, most of which were accounted for by Beetles. The effects of an expansion programme which had begun when the company was taken over by Thomas Tilling in 1957 were undoubtedly being felt.

By 1968 vw GB Ltd were the largest foreign importers in the UK. Much of the credit for this achievement can be attributed to J. J. Graydon who retired from the company in January of that year. Alan Dix, who had had a highly successful career with vw in the United States, took over as managing director with a brief to completely restructure the UK operation.

Many of the problems which confronted Dix had dogged the company almost since birth: inefficiency, poor standards of workmanship,

165

apathy amongst staff and primitive conditions, to name but a few. Amongst the measures taken was the phasing-out of the twenty-seven distributors, allowing vw direct contact with the dealers. New standards were laid down for almost every aspect of sales and service and dealers who failed to toe the line were replaced with others willing to cooperate with the company. The effect was a drastic reduction in the number of dealers from just over 400 to just under 300. The restructuring, when completed, produced a highly efficient organisation run with almost military precision.

In 1973 Britain celebrated the 250,000th Beetle to be imported since 1953, and to mark the occasion 25,000 special GT Beetles were produced complete with £100 worth of extras.

In 1975 the company was purchased from Thomas Tilling by the Lohnro group of companies, and Mr Michael Heelas, formerly managing director of Mercedes-Benz in Britain, took over as managing director.

Michael Heelas had taken over from John Wagner who, during two and a half years with the company, had been involved in a major re-organisation when the vw subsidiary, Audi-NSU, was merged with vw GB. This meant that most vw dealers and most NSU dealers would in future sell and service both ranges of vehicles. This required re-training of staff and investment in new equipment and premises, but by 1975 when John Wagner left the foundation was laid for a whole new success-ful chapter in the history of vw GB.

Beetle sales, however, after reaching an all-time high in 1972 with a total of 35,525, started to go into decline. The combined effects of the sterling crisis, the revaluation of the German Mark, higher production costs and the oil crisis, resulted in an escalation in Beetle prices. For example, a 1300 De Luxe cost £684 in 1970, whereas the 1200L in 1977 cost £2,626, a rise of almost 400 per cent within the space of seven years. Sales in 1974 dropped to almost half the 15,442 of the previous year, in 1975 they plummeted to 5,494, in 1976 to 1,073, and in 1977 to just 492, with a final batch of 540 for 1978.

At the same time as Beetle sales were on the decline, Wolfsburg were introducing their new range of front-engined, water-cooled models, which quickly caught on in Britain.

166

It was now becoming quite clear that the writing was on the wall for the Beetle in Britain. The faithful old friend, so abused in its early years in Britain, but which had since found its way to over a quarter of a million owners, ceased to be imported in 1977. The last batch of cars was shipped to Britain in that year, to the chagrin of the faithful followers, many of whom will undoubtedly remain faithful to the marque for many years to come.

Today, with distribution being made directly to the dealers by the company, enviably high standards have been attained by the vw dealer network in the UK. As well as Ramsgate, modern warehouses were built at Trowbridge, Doncaster, Whitburn and Edenbridge, but these are now all replaced by the new warehouse at Milton Keynes. Ramsgate and Grimsby are the main ports of entry for Volkswagens sold in Britain. They are brought across the channel from Emden and Antwerp in modern purpose-built, 'roll-on-roll-off' vessels with up to 500 vehicles in each shipment.

The new range of cars and the successors to the air-cooled range have been decisive factors in opening up a new era for Volkswagen in the UK, where the selling and servicing of vws and Audis today give employment to more than 10,000 people. Operations are now being directed from their new headquarters at Milton Keynes in Buckinghamshire, first inaugurated in 1977. This houses the company's administrative offices and a highly sophisticated computer centre with a technical school which will eventually train 5,000 staff from the national dealer network. The site also houses the enormous warehouse which covers 5 acres (2 hectares) and contains a staggering 40,000 parts worth some £15,000,000, the entire complex employing a total of 450 people.

7

The Beetle in the USA

When Nordhoff returned from the States in 1949, without even a hint of any future for the Beetle in the world's biggest car market, little could he have envisaged the day when Porsche's creation would be seen on every main avenue and freeway, from New York City to San Francisco, providing transport for people as diverse as the multitude of nationalities which make up this motor-car orientated society.

Save for a few Beetles taken back by ex-servicemen upon completing their tour of duty in Germany, it was 1950 before the Beetle made its début in the States in any quantity, via Max Hoffman of New York. This was merely one further addition to his wide range of foreign cars, including that other now-famous make, Porsche. Only 352 Beetles sold in that year, plus a few in late 1949—sales of a positively miniscule nature—which served to emphasise the problems that would have to be faced before any kind of success could be envisaged.

To the American citizen the car from Wolfsburg was tarnished with the memories of wartime press jibes about 'Hitler's car', and in one case a cartoon depicted the Beetle with a machine gun protruding through the front windscreen. Another major obstacle, was the general mistrust of small cars, born out of the unfortunate experiences of those who had previously opted for smaller-engined vehicles as a cheap alternative, but short engine-life and generally mediocre performance had driven many of these cost-conscious individuals back to the larger and more traditional variety of car, where at least high fuel consumption was offset to some degree by the longer life of the engine.

The British were amongst the first to begin post-war exports to the States, followed by a number of other European manufacturers, but poor back-up facilities, including the availability of spares, and general after-sales care just exacerbated small-car prejudices.

This was also the beginning of an era when American motoring eccentricities demanded progressively bigger automobiles, with heavily chromed external ornamentation, and power units which grew in size with each passing year, if only to compensate for the rapidly extending bodywork both fore and aft. Following the automobile starvation of the war years, the glittering monsters of the 'fifties became the American public's number one adult plaything and status symbol.

The Beetle, or Bug, as it became more popularly known in the States, smelt of anything but luxury; its unorthodox appearance and design merely gave rise to suspicion, and its very approach to motoring was completely out of keeping with American motoring trends. All in all the Beetle's prospects in the States looked rather bleak.

To Max Hoffman the Beetle was just another foreign car, and he had little interest in the Beetle other than its immediate sales potential.

After a further two years of fearfully disappointing sales—367 in 1951 plus 50 transporters, rising slightly to 887 in 1952 with 93 transporters— Wolfsburg stepped in. In late 1953 Hoffman's franchise was cancelled and vw headquarters were set up in New York and San Francisco. These two centres controlled the eastern and western states respectively, with the Mississippi River reportedly acting as the dividing line between the two.

When rumours grew of the impending doom of the Hoffman vw operation distributors set up direct links with Wolfsburg and this resulted in quite a number of these distributors finding themselves both importers and distributors. The result was a hotchpotch network of independent vw operators, devoid of any uniform standard or approach to sales and service, with the two headquarters acting as little more than company representatives.

Wolfsburg's next move took place on 19 April 1955, when they established a new subsidiary called Volkswagen of America with headquarters on Fifth Avenue, New York. It later moved to new premises at Englewood Cliffs, New Jersey, designed specifically for supplying and exploiting the vw market in the USA.

169

Beetle sales for 1955 jumped fourfold over the previous year to 32,662 plus 3,189 transporters.

The marked improvement in sales was certainly, in part, attributable to the joint efforts of Wolfsburg's representatives and the more energetic of the vw distributors and dealers. But it was the Beetle itself which, in the States, had the task of proving itself to a discerning motoring public, in contrast to the early post-war days in Europe when it was supplying cars to a continent suffering from an acute shortage of vehicles. However, those in the States who did become Beetle owners soon developed admiration and respect for the little car from Germany, and the Beetle's reputation for reliability spread more by word of mouth than official exhortation, as advertising other than showroom sales-literature was almost non-existent at that time.

However much punishment was meted out by over-enthusiastic owners the Beetle just seemed to survive, justifying Professor Porsche's determination that small cars should be designed as such, and not as a scaled-down compromise version of a larger vehicle. Backed by what was considered to be a highly advanced design, even in the later 'fifties the Beetle was to stand head and shoulders above its other small-car competitors trying to gain a footing in the American market and, in total defiance of its American adversaries, the Beetle carved out its reputation.

However, as Nordhoff insisted, a car is only as good as its after-sales service, and with many of the American dealerships a general lack of well-organised after-sales care led to sloppy repairs, often carried out under primitive conditions using poorly trained staff with totally inadequate or unbalanced stocks. In 1956, therefore, Wolfsburg sent over a team of fully trained mechanics and spare-parts representatives to tour the entire American vw network in a fleet of vans, with the aim of raising the general standard of repairs, maintenance and availability of spare parts, with new schools being set up by the distributors for retraining mechanics from the dealers.

Plans put forward in 1955 to build the Beetle in the States were later abandoned on account of gross underestimations in costs. Instead, vw arranged for long-term leases on ocean-going freighters for the fourteen-

170

day journey from the German ports of Bremen and Hamburg to various ports of entry around the United States.

By 1957 the numbers of dealers had grown to 350, with Beetle sales for that year totalling 54,189 plus 18,366 transporters, rising again the following year to 61,507 Beetles and 24,478 transporters.

It is certainly true to say that since Max Hoffman took delivery of the first batch of Beetles in 1950 the car had come a long way by the late 'fifties, with a marked improvement in the general standards amongst the dealers. However, total vw sales in the us still only accounted for a small proportion of the total sales of cars there. In 1959, therefore, Nordhoff, who was far from happy with this situation, sent over one of his most respected right-hand men, Carl Hahn, to take charge of the situation and iron out all the bugs in the American operation.

Before taking over as head of vw in the States in January 1959, Carl Hahn had worked in Wolfsburg's export sales department, and before this he had worked for a while as Nordhoff's personal assistant. It was his flair for the sales and promotional side of the business that led to him ultimately being chosen for the task of putting vw on a par with the American motoring giants. With a brief from Nordhoff to expand the dealer network and modernise the entire us operation, Hahn began work on 5 January. By the end of that year the number of dealers had increased to almost 500, and sales in 1960 rose to 127,159 Beetles and 34,878 transporters.

The car's popularity during the late 'fifties outstripped authorised dealer deliveries, which led to a Beetle black market. Foreign agents shipped the cars through various ports in small numbers and distributed them to non-vw agents as sidelines to their normal stocks. This included dealers of other well-known foreign makes, plus a number of second-hand car dealers. The estimated total of unauthorised sales during this period seems to have accounted for up to 20 per cent of new vws but it steadily decreased with the expansion in the number of vw dealers.

In 1959 Hahn commissioned two advertising agencies for the purposes of launching vw's first national advertising campaign. Whilst one handled the Beetle, the other took the transporter range. Up until this time vws had never been featured in any national advertising

2 shapes known the world over.

Nobody notices Coke bottles or Volkswagens any more.

They're so well known, they blend in with the scenery.

It doesn't matter what the scenery is, either. You can walk in and buy a VW in any one of 136 countries.

And that takes in lots of scenery.

Deserts. Mountains. Hot places. Cold places. Volkswagens thrive.

Hot and cold don't matter; the VW engine is air-cooled. It doesn't use water, so it can't freeze up or boil over.

And having the engine in the back is what makes all the difference when it comes to mud and sand and snow.

The weight is over the power wheels and so the traction is terrific.

VWs also get along so well wherever they are because the service is as good in Tasmania as it is in Toledo.

(The only reason you can't buy a VW at the North Pole is that Volkswagen won't sell you one. There's no VW service around the corner.)

We hear that it's possible to buy yourself a Coke at the North Pole, though.

Which makes us suspect there's only one thing that can get through ahead of a Volkswagen.

A Coke truck.

Dealer Name

VW 2579-71

Two of the advertisements which boosted the Beetle's US sales in 1959–62.

The $35,000 Volkswagen.

Have we gone stark raving mad?

No, but when we heard this car was on display at the Los Angeles International Auto Show, we thought somebody had.

As it turned out, there was a method to the owner's madness.

Why not transform the world's best known economy car into the world's most economical limousine?

After all, a lot of the things that make great luxury cars great are already there in the humble little Bug:

Like 23 years of perfecting every single part of the car.

And subjecting it to over 16,000 different inspections before we sell it to you.

And having it worth lots of money to you when you sell it to someone else.

So why not stretch it out to limo length?

Why not add an intercom, bar and mahogany woodwork and tufted English upholstery and a carriage lamp to signal the doorman?

 Why not be the savingest millionaire on the road?

That, children, is exactly how the rich get richer.

VW 2572-71

173

whatsoever, but what followed during the period 1959-61 was a long series of witty and original advertisements extolling the Beetle, many of which have passed into the legends of American vw history. This created a boost in sales and a string of awards for what, at that time, was considered almost unique advertising.

What had previously been looked upon as little or no threat to the American motoring giants was beginning, by the late 'fifties, as Beetle sales began to gain momentum, to take on an increasingly menacing look. The craze for chrome, and yet more chrome, and bigger and better, was beginning to wane, as the American motoring public began to awaken to this cripplingly expensive and highly ludicrous method of establishing their social status, and a more rational approach to motoring began to emerge. There can be no doubt that the Beetle played its part in helping to shape a more down-to-earth approach to motoring, with American car owners not only opting for cheaper and more practical vehicles, giving easier parking, lower fuel consumption, and smaller garages—in fact, you could get two Beetles into the same space previously occupied by one car—but also, and probably even more significant, superior after-sales care, something which had tended to take second place in the rush to satisfy the us public's appetite for swanky automobiles. They had also noticed that the latest Beetle looked just the same as its ancestors, whether five, ten, or more years old, doing away with the need to change models before they became too out-of-date, with the consequent loss in its trade-in value.

In 1960 Detroit was answering back to the threat posed by its foreign rival with a new generation of compact cars, including the 1960 Chevrolet Corvair, which featured a 6-cylinder, flat-four, rear, air-cooled, aluminium engine, with all-round independent suspension, and a noted absence of bright metal trimmings; in fact a car which left no one in any doubt as to which model it was meant to compete with.

The effect of Detroit's thrust into the small-car market was a 50 per cent reduction in foreign-car sales, but vw sales were left completely unscathed. In fact, contrary to the hopes and aims of its American competitors, it actually gained from the misfortunes of its foreign rivals. As quickly as the new American compacts made their début on the motoring scene, the inevitable happened, and the small cars aimed at undermining the Beetle and other small cars progressively grew in size with each passing year. vw was left to pick up an even greater share of the foreign small-car market, lost to its competitors during the initial American counter-attack—which had almost fizzled out by the mid 'sixties—and it actually went on to outsell the domestic small cars.

In 1958 Nordhoff went to the States to receive the Elmer A. Sperry award on behalf of his company and Professor Ferdinand Porsche—an award posthumously bestowed by three American engineering societies in recognition of vw's contribution to transportation. He returned there again in 1962 for the celebration to mark the millionth vw, not counting the black-market contingent, to be sold in the States. Nordhoff must have felt proud of such outstanding achievements and the trips must have brought back memories of his lone visit to the States in 1949 when he received the cold shoulder from the New York car pundits who looked on the Beetle as little more than a joke.

When Carl Hahn returned home to Germany in 1964, he left behind him a highly organised, super-efficient and fully fledged distributor-dealer network, with Beetle sales which, since he had first taken over in 1959, had risen almost three times to 276,187—in fact, almost 70 per cent of the American foreign-car market.

During Hahn's stay the distributor and dealer network had been the subject of radical change, with a greater emphasis on service. A strict set of rules were laid down to ensure that individual dealers carried sufficient stock and adequate servicing facilities for the number of vehicles in the dealer's area, and also for premises and staff conditions. This resulted in a standardised approach to buildings and provided that familiar vw garage image with roomy, well-lit showrooms and adequately laid-out service areas, operated by clean, overalled and well-qualified staff who were retrained at new schools set up by the distributors. By 1963 the number of staff employed by Volkswagen of America had expanded from the original three to over 250, and by 1965 the number of dealerships had increased to 900.

With an organisation now modelled on the one in Germany, Beetle sales increased rapidly from 314,625 in 1965, plus 37,796 transporters, to 423,008 in 1968, plus 50,756 transporters. Sadly this was to be the last time that such figures would be attained and (as explained in chapter 5) sales for the Beetle went henceforth into decline. Transporter sales followed suit after 1970, when they dropped to 65,069. Type 3 sales to the States, which began in 1965, reached 4,725 for that year, increased to 57,954 the following year, to 99,012 in 1970 and then began a yearly decline along with the rest of the air-cooled range.

Since Volkswagen's recovery after the war, the Beetle's long career has included innumerable triumphs, often against almost insuperable odds, but its success in the United States must undoubtedly rate as its finest achievement. When Porsche's creation first entered the American motoring arena, it was viewed with the utmost scepticism, and was treated initially by the majority of people as nothing more than a joke on four wheels. However, the Beetle survived to become the country's number one small car which, by the time of its demise in the showrooms, had reached total sales, since its introduction in 1949, of well in excess of 5 million.

Beetle mania (often referred to in Beetle circles as being 'bitten by the Bug') has never been more openly displayed than by its American fans. The devotion of many of its keen followers there has bordered on the fanatical. They are able to share their enthusiasm with fellow Beetle buffs through the multitude of clubs devoted to the marque, and the entire movement is orchestrated by the Volkswagen Club of America, the world's largest VW club, whose monthly magazine, *Small World*, and quarterly magazine, VW *Autoist*, between them provide a wide variety of VW news, club events and galas, and technical information, plus a host of other items of interest to its readers. The addiction to Volkswagen is the same whether it is a new 'Rabbit', a transporter, or that noisy little car which has won its way into the hearts of countless American citizens. A number of Bug fanatics own more than one Beetle and sometimes entire families whose members are old enough to drive have been 'bitten by the Bug'; many of them will undoubtedly remain faithful to the marque for a good many years to come.

In 1969, when the devaluation of the dollar began to hit Beetle sales, Wolfsburg had to face the agonising problem of finding a successor for the now ageing Beetle. They had to find a car capable of regaining at least some of those massive losses created by the drop-off in Beetle sales, and able to match not only the latest American offerings but, probably far more important, the new range of small cars coming from the Japanese. By the early 'seventies the latter were already making inroads into the American small-car market, at a time when Wolfsburg's new range was still either in prototype or pre-production form. Wolfsburg's massive investment programme of the late 'sixties and early 'seventies, however, culminated in a range of new cars which has since proved second to none, and has provided the company with a worthy successor to the Beetle, capable of filling the gap left by the Beetle in the American market.

The 'Rabbit' (the official American title for the 'Golf'), since its introduction into the States in 1974 when just fifty-eight were sold, has provided the discerning American motorist with a car which fully satisfied everyone's small-car needs, and has steadily revived the company's flagging fortunes in what was once its most lucrative market.

At an opening ceremony attended by Wolfsburg's chief, Tony Schmucker and the president of Volkswagen of America, Stuart Perkins—the extremely able successor to Carl Hahn—plus many of vw's top personnel both from the United States and elsewhere, the first Rabbit came off the production line. The venue was the brand new vw factory at Westmoreland, New Stanton, Pennsylvania, part of a new Volkswagen subsidiary called Volkswagen Manufacturing Corporation of America (vwmoa), incorporated in Pennsylvania, with James McLernon, formerly manufacturing manager of General Motors, Chevrolet division, becoming its first president.

Justification for this latter move lay in the impressive sales record for the previously imported Rabbit which, by the time the first cars began rolling off the new American production line, had already passed the quarter million mark. (World-wide sales had by now reached 2 million.) Capable of 0-60mph (96.6kph) in 11.8 seconds, and a top speed of 100mph (161kph), plus a thrifty fuel consumption of 38mpg ($13\frac{1}{2}$km per litre) on the open highway, and 25mpg (9km per litre) in the city, its success comes as little surprise, and the diesel-engined version of the car, which was phased in during 1979, provides even greater economy. Backed by 1,000 US dealers, with their strict adherence to Volkswagen's fully comprehensive and first-class after-sales service, the front-engined, water-cooled Rabbit looks set to break records of its own, and to carry forward into the 'eighties the banner of success first raised by its air-cooled predecessor.

APPENDICES

I
Ferdinand Porsche

Although Professor Porsche was in his seventies after the war, his career was by no means over. Soon after peace was made the French invited him to build a small car on the lines of the Beetle but nothing came of this. His early interest in sports cars was, however, to be fulfilled in the marque bearing his family name. The Porsche car, as is well known, had success as a private car, in competitions and in racing.

Professor Porsche with his nephew and faithful secretary, Ghislaine Kaes, on Austria's Gross-Glockner in September 1950, just a few months before Porsche's death. Today Ghislaine Kaes, as company archivist and historian, continues his lifetime of dedication to a cause for which he claims inspiration from a man who died almost thirty years ago, and anyone having met him would be reluctant to disagree.

181

Its five outright wins at Le Mans between 1970 and 1979, six first in the World Master Championships and eight wins in the Imsa series are some of its notable achievements. And the original Porsche consultancy, which moved to a modern design centre in Weissach in 1972, still prospers under his son's control.

When Professor Porsche died in 1951 he had seen his brainchild, the Beetle, well on the road to its worldwide success and, in spite of the triumphs of the other car bearing the family name, perhaps his proudest moment of all was when he visited Wolfsburg shortly before his death to see his great vw creation coming off the production line.

2

Models Available

The Beetle remained almost unaltered since it first went into production in 1946 up until 1949, and it was not until the introduction of the first export model in that year that any significant changes began to take place.

Quite a number of modifications carried out in the late 'sixties and early 'seventies were the direct result of new safety regulations and anti-pollution measures introduced under US Federal law. (Exhaust emission was to be controlled, and there were also plans to enforce the introduction of air bags—something which certainly caused VW and the American motor manufacturers some worry.) In many instances these measures resulted in special US models with items not present on European models or only available as extras.

Nor were all other models available in every country. For example, only the De-Luxe version of the 1200 was exported to the USA before 1965, and after 1965, only the 1300. Subsequently only the most powerful-engined models, namely the 1500, the 1302S and the 1303S, plus in the 'seventies a basic 1600, were exported to the US. The UK, on the other hand, sported a wide range, particularly in the 'seventies, but even this did not include some of the many varieties and numerous specials which were currently available in Germany. The Cabriolet introduced by Karmann of Osnabrück in 1949 was, and always has been, based on the most luxurious and powerful Beetle in the range, the De Luxe, up until 1963, then on the 1300, the 1500, the 1302S, the 1303S and finally the LS. The basic and rather austere Standard model 1200 which ran concurrently with the De-Luxe until 1964, appears to have been more popular in Germany than elsewhere, such as the UK, where crash gear gearboxes and mechanical brakes were associated more with pre-war models. Not surprisingly, it was never introduced into the US or Canada. Countries such as Brazil, Mexico and South Africa, where Beetles were built locally, began to produce their own models with different names from those found in Europe. In South Africa, for example, the 1976 range consisted of a 1300, a 1600 'Super Bug', a 1600L—roughly equivalent to the American basic 1600 Custom model—and finally a sporty model called the 1600SP with twin carburettors, elaborate instrumentation and racing trim. In Brazil the mid-seventies range consisted of a 1300, and a 1600 similar to the South African 1600L, but the majority of modifications carried out on the German-built cars were duplicated on Beetles built around the world.

MODELS AVAILABLE IN THE UK

Model year

1953–64	Standard/De Luxe/Cabriolet
1965	1200/1200A/Cabriolet
1966	1200A (special order only) /1300/1300 Cabriolet
1967	1300/1500/1500 Cabriolet (1200 not available that year)
1968–70	New 1200/1300/1500/1500 Cabriolet
1971	1200/1300/1600 (1302S) Super Beetle/1302/1302S Cabriolet
1972	1200/1300/1302S (special order only) 1302S Cabriolet
1973	1200/1300/1300A/1303/1303S/1303S Cabriolet
1974	1200/Jeans Beetle/1300A/City Beetle/1300/GT Beetle/1303/1303S/1600
1975	1200/1300/1303
1976–7	1200L/1303LS Cabriolet (reintroduced after being dropped from UK range in 1973)
1978	1200L discontinued/1303LS Cabriolet continues
1979	Cabriolet discontinued

MODELS AVAILABLE IN THE USA

This list does not include the countless specials produced all over the

184

United States in special promotions over the years, but only those cars imported from Germany.

Model year

1949–65	De-Luxe 1200/1200 Cabriolet
1965	1300/1300 Cabriolet
1966–9	1500/1500 Cabriolet
1969	1600/1600 Cabriolet
1970–2	1302S Super Bug/Standard 1600 Custom Beetle/1302S Cabriolet
1972	1303S/Standard 1600 Beetle/Sports Bug
1973–5	1303S/Standard 1600 Beetle/1303LS Cabriolet
1975–7	1303S/Standard 1600 Beetle/1303LS Cabriolet/La Grande Bug
1977	1303S discontinued/1303LS continues
1978	1303LS Cabriolet only
1979	1303LS discontinued

3
Notable Modifications to Models

The following lists should provide a useful outline to the various Beetle models, revealing the vast number of improvements that have been carried out on the car over a period of almost thirty years and the wide range of models that have been produced. The information listed here has been limited to the lesser technical improvements, as a complete list would fill a large volume and would be only fully understood by the more technically minded.

Until 1955 the model year began on 1 January, but from 1955 onwards models for the following year were announced at the beginning of August, generally on the 1st, so that, for example, 1956 models were announced on 1 August 1955. Further modifications were also frequently carried out during the course of the model year.

1949 MODEL YEAR

Models available: Standard; De-Luxe or Export (introduced on 1 July with much improved gloss paintwork and extras not available on the more basic Standard model); Cabriolet (introduced by Karmann of Osnabrück, being open version of De-Luxe).

Standard model Available in blue/grey only.
De-Luxe/Standard/Cabriolet Front hood opens from inside by cable release with new grab handle replacing locking handle on front hood. Licence-plate indentation deleted on engine lid. Specially designed Solex carburettor introduced as standard equipment. Starting-crank bracket with guide-hole bracket on rear bumper discontinued.
De-Luxe/Cabriolet More plush seating with arm rests at front and rear.

Option of radio or clock in nearside panel on facia. Ashtrays front and rear. New, single-spoke steering wheel. Ivory-coloured, instrument-panel controls and gear-selector knob. Horn moved from front to new position under wing (some had twin horns flared into the wings). Chrome strip mouldings added to waist along body sides. Choice of colours.

1950 MODEL YEAR

Models available: Standard model; De-Luxe; Cabriolet/Sunshine-roof model (consisting of a roll-back, cloth-fabric roof—not a special model, but merely an extra available on either the De-Luxe or Standard).

All Models Noise dampers added to heater ducts. Thermostatically controlled throttle ring added to air intake on engine-cooling fan housing to prevent over-cooling particularly in cold weather. Fuel-mixture heating device added. Vent window added to rear passengers' windows.
De-Luxe/Cabriolet Hydraulic brakes replace former mechanical brakes (Standard model retains mechanical brakes).

1951 MODEL YEAR

Models available: Standard; De-Luxe; Cabriolet.

All models Vent windows in rear passengers' windows replaced by vent flaps in front quarter panels.
De-Luxe/Cabriolet Wolfsburg crest added to front hood directly above grab handle. Chrome trim added around front windshield.

1952 MODEL YEAR

Models available: Standard; De-Luxe; Cabriolet.

All models Vent flaps deleted from front quarter panels and replaced by vent windows in front side windows. Loop-type handle on engine lid replaced with T-type handle. Combined brake and tail lights with orange window in top of tail-light housing, in place of earlier single light in centre of engine lid. Tyre sizes altered from 5.00X 16 to 5.60X 15. Bumpers and over-riders modified for greater strength. Larger windshield-heater defrosting vents. Handbrake fitted with rubber boot to reduce draughts. Former heating-control pull-knob replaced with rotary knob. Improved seat backs with stronger springing. Window-crank operation reduced from $10\frac{1}{2}$ turns to $3\frac{1}{2}$ turns. New-style instrument control panel with single glove compartment with lid, and control lamps situated in speedometer housing. Direction indicator moved from control panel to steering column. Interior light fitted above nearside door pillar. Faster, self-parking windshield wipers covering larger wiper area. More rounded rear-view mirror replaces square type. Carburettor fitted with accelerator pump to eliminate flat spots when engine is cold. Six-leaf torsion bars on front suspension at top and bottom, and smaller-diameter torsion bars fitted to rear giving smoother ride with less vibration.

De-Luxe/Cabriolet Syncromesh added to second, third and fourth gears. (Standard model retains crash gearbox.)

1953 MODEL YEAR

Models available: Standard; De-Luxe; Cabriolet.

All models Oval, one-piece rear window replaces split rear window. Eight-leaf front torsion bars fitted to top and bottom for increased longevity. Lock button on front vent windows. Brake-fluid reservoir moved from earlier position at master cylinder to behind spare wheel under front hood. More effective heating achieved by deleting heater outlets near to back seat. Generator output stepped up from 130 to 160 watts.

De-Luxe /Cabriolet Trim mouldings made of anti-corrosive alloy.

1954 MODEL YEAR

Models available: Standard; De-Luxe; Cabriolet.

All models Engine capacity increased from 1131cc to 1192cc and compression ratio raised from 30bhp (SAE) to 36bhp (SAE) at maximum 3,700rpm. Oil-bath air cleaner replaces felt element filter. Vacuum-advance control fitted to distributor, giving improved performance without raising fuel consumption. Top window in tail-light housing dropped, replaced by double-filament, tail/brake light bulbs with re-designed lens, more visible to drivers behind. Engine break-in period no longer necessary. Combined starter and ignition switch replaces separate starter button on instrument panel. Seat backrests made narrower to permit increased leg room for rear passengers. Back-seat backrest held in position by rubber strip. Improved upholstery.

1956 MODEL YEAR (begins August 1955)

Models available: Standard; De-Luxe; Cabriolet.

All models Twin chrome exhaust pipes replace former single pipe (black enamel on Standard model). Tail lights moved 2in higher on rear wings. Redesigned fuel tank creates increased luggage area under front hood. Cranked gear lever replaces straight type and is moved forward for easier operation—which also enables heater-control knob to be moved forward on tunnel for easier access. Wider front seats, increased by 1¼in, now adjustable for three positions of rake. Rear seats repositioned giving 2in increased space in rear passenger compartment. Width between doors slightly increased. Horizontal steering spoke moved to off-centre position for improved handling and unobstructed view of instrument panel.

Sunshine-roof model PVC sunroof replaces cloth fabric.

USA De-Luxe Flashing direction indicators mounted low down on front and rear wings in place of semaphore type. Bumper over rider bows added to front and rear bumpers.

1957 MODEL YEAR (begins August 1956)

Models available: Standard; De-Luxe; Cabriolet.

All models Improved heater distribution achieved by moving heater outlets back nearer doors, with heater channels placed in side members. Adjustable striker plates on doors. Damp-resistant sound-proofing material fitted in engine compartment.

1958 MODEL YEAR (begins August 1957)

Models available: Standard; De-Luxe; Cabriolet.

All models Larger rear window replaces former oval type, increasing window area by 95 per cent. Front windshield area increased by 17 per cent. Re-shaped engine lid for improved arrangement for lighting of licence plate, now fitted with dish-shaped lens and larger lamp bulb. Water drainage below rear air intake for greater protection of engine compartment. Wider front brake drums and shoes with larger front and rear-brake cylinders. Larger rear-view interior mirror. Sun visor reshaped to match contour of windshield (De-Luxe models only). Roller-type accelerator pedal replaced with flat treadle type for easier operation. Redesigned instrument panel, with larger glove compartment and ashtray mounted on facia, now places radio grille in front of driver. Leatherette seat coverings and door trim replace cloth fabric (for better wear). Larger windshield-wiper blades with swept area increased by 35 per cent.
Cabriolet Front-windshield area increased by 8 per cent, and rear window by 45 per cent, requiring modified air intake on engine lid to be reduced from single row of vertical louvres to twin horizontal inlets on engine lid.

1959 MODEL YEAR (begins August 1958)

Models available: Standard; De-Luxe; Cabriolet.

All models Strengthened chassis. Improved fan belt. Stronger clutch springs.

1960 MODEL YEAR (begins August 1959)

Models available: Standard; De-Luxe; Cabriolet.

De-Luxe Anti-roll bar fitted to front suspension for improved cornering and general handling. Transparent green visor replaced with padded visor. Dished steering wheel replaces former flat horizontal-spoke type. More comfortable contoured front-seat backs. Passenger armrest on door recessed for easier door opening. Rigid door handles replaced by pull-out type. Foot rest added on passenger's side.

All models Generator output increased from 160 watts to 180 watts. Self-cancelling direction-indicator switch.

1961 MODEL YEAR (begins August 1960)

Models available: Standard; De-Luxe; Cabriolet.

De-Luxe Engine compression ratio raised from 6.6 to 7.0, increasing output from 36bhp (SAE) to 40.5bhp (SAE) at maximum 3,900rpm. Hydraulic steering damper added for steadier steering. Syncromesh added on all forward gears (previously second, third and fourth only). Automatic choke introduced. Sun visor and grab handle added on passenger's side. Asymmetrical headlamps introduced, providing increased illumination distance to nearside kerb (not fitted to US model).

All models Flashing direction indicators replace former semaphore type, with new twin-compartment rear lights. Non-repeat starter switch introduced, preventing risk of damage to starter pinion. Transparent brake-fluid reservoir for easy checking. Front luggage area increased by 65 per cent by redesigning fuel tank. Improved slimmer gear-change lever. Door-key slots changed from horizontal to vertical. Pump-type windshield washers.

1962 MODEL YEAR (begins August 1961)

Models available: Standard; De-Luxe; Cabriolet.

All models New larger three-piece tail light incorporating flashers and reflectors. Maintenance-free clutch and handbrake cables. Door checks allow doors to stay open for added convenience. Larger front-seat runners allow increased leg room. Seat-belt mounting points added. Exterior driving mirror added. Adjustable sliding covers on heater vents. Spring-loaded front hood makes for easier lifting and greater safety. Single heater vent added to rear footwell.

De-Luxe Steering mechanism changed from worm and nut to worm and roller for general improvement in steering and wear. Compressed-air windshield washers replace former pump type with easier and more effective operation. Reserve 2-gallon fuel tap replaced by fuel gauge mounted on dash.

1963 MODEL YEAR (begins August 1962)

Models available: Standard; De-Luxe; Cabriolet.

All models Modified engine-cooling fan and housing for improved heating. Increased floor insulation. Leatherette headliner replaces cloth-fabric. Nylon window guides.

De-Luxe Wolfsburg crest on front hood deleted.

Cabriolet Rear window area increased by one-third.

1964 MODEL YEAR (begins August 1963)

Models available: Standard, De-Luxe; Cabriolet.

All models Vinyl seat coverings replace former non-porous leatherette. Half-ring horn replaced by thumb-push type. Wider licence-plate light-housing.

Sunshine roof model Cloth-fabric sun-roof replaced with steel sliding roof operated by a crank handle situated above front windshield.

1965 MODEL YEAR (begins August 1964)

Models available: 1200 (De-Luxe now generally referred to as 1200); 1200A; Cabriolet.

1200A Replaces old austere Standard model as the new basic model for the 1965 model year. Retains old 36bhp engine; now fitted with hydraulic brakes. Full syncromesh gearbox, steering damper, stabiliser, visor, three-spoke steering wheel with centre round horn-push side moulding strip, chromed external parts and bumpers, vinyl seat covering and choice of colours.

Cabriolet Continues as open version of 1200 until following year.

All models Front windshield area increased by 19.5 per cent with slightly deeper side windows, increased by 1in, with slimmer door and window pillars. Press-button lock on engine lid. Heater rotary-control knob replaced by twin pull-up levers mounted on tunnel for separate control of front and rear heater vents. Longer windshield-wiper blades, now parked on left. New and more easily operated front-vent window-fasteners. Rear-seat back now folds forward to give increased luggage area.

1966 MODEL YEAR (begins August 1965)

Models available: 1200A; 1300; 1300 Cabriolet.

1300 New introduction with 1285cc engine (also fitted to 1300 Cabriolet), compression ratio 7.3:1, giving maximum output of 50bhp (SAE) at 4,600rpm. Replaces 1200 in USA.

1200A Available in UK on special order fitted with 41.5bhp engine.

1300/1200A Improved front suspension. (Wider spacing between front torsion bars with improved front shock-absorbers.) 1300 badge on engine lid. Central heater outlet added to front windshield. Reversion to half-circular horn ring (1200A retains three-spoke central-horn type). New safety front-seat backrest locking device. Three-in-one, dip-switch/flasher direction-indicator lever on steering column.

1967 MODEL YEAR (begins August 1966)

Models available: 1300; 1500 (newly introduced); 1500 Cabriolet (newly introduced); (1200 deleted from 1967 model year in UK).

1500/1500 Cabriolet 1493cc engine. Compression ratio 7.5:1 and maximum output 53bhp (SAE) at 4,200rpm. Front disc brakes. Reshaped engine lid which enables licence plate to be mounted in vertical position. 1500 badge on engine lid. Supersedes 1300 in USA.
1500 Rear track increased to 53.1in.
1300 Rear track increased to 53.5in.
1300/1500 New pre-heat system—warm air from engine compartment transferred by flexible heater hoses and mixed with carburettor air intake for easier start in cold weather. Shorter engine lid. Slimmer chrome trim along sides. New safety rotary locks preventing doors bursting open on crash impact.
1500 US model Drum brakes still retained at front and rear. Head restraint combined with front backrests. Parking lights integrated into front signal-indicator housing. Reversing (back-up) lights mounted on rear bumper.

1968 MODEL YEAR (begins August 1967)

Models available: 1200; 1300; 1500; 1500 Cabriolet.

1200 New and improved with wider track (same as 1300), new pre-heat system (same as 1300), chromed bumpers, side moulding strips, vinyl seat coverings, front ashtray and windshield-defroster outlets. Although very much superior to previous basic 1200 models, the new 1200 remains at the bottom of the range as the only 1200-engined Beetle available, *less* the following items fitted to the more luxurious 1300 and 1500 models: armrest, two assist straps, grab handle on passenger side, door pocket, ashtray in rear, two-speed wipers, headlight flasher, door-operated courtesy light, fuel gauge integrated into speedometer dial, fresh-air ventilation systems, safety-locking backrest. Engine remains identical to that fitted to 1200A with 41.5bhp at 3,900rpm.

All models New vertical position for headlights (introduced in USA in previous model year). Collapsible steering column to reduce injury in case of accidents. New door handles with inside trigger release. Fuel-tank filler neck moved from inside front hood to outside, behind flap on front quarter panel. Shorter gear lever and handbrake.

1300/1500 Electrical system changed from 6 to 12 volt (introduced in USA in previous model year). Dual braking system with front and rear operating independently to eliminate the risk of total brake failure (introduced in USA in previous model year). New-style stronger bumpers, mounted slightly higher. Two-speed wipers. Fresh-air ventilation system with air drawn in through louvres high up on front hood, controlled by knobs mounted on dashboard.

1500 Semi-automatic stickshift model introduced with double-jointed rear axle. A clutch-free operation with four-stage speed-range selector, by means of hydrodynamic torque converter; automatic clutch and gear-type transmission. USA model with exhaust-emission control system fitted and Federal Standards Certificate mounted on front door post.

1969 MODEL YEAR (begins August 1968)

Models available: 1200; 1300; 1500; 1500 Cabriolet.

All models Front-hood release located in glove compartment. Warning lights in speedo housing identified by letters or symbols. Locking fuel-tank flap operated by lever under off-side of dash. Front-heater outlets moved back under doors.

1300 Now available with semi-automatic stickshift.

1300/1500 Combined ignition switch and steering lock on steering column. Audio emergency flasher system. (Pull-out knob on dash activates all four direction indicators simultaneously.)

1500 USA version with electrically heated rear window (defogger). Day-and-night rear-view mirror.

1970 MODEL YEAR (begins August 1969)

Models available: 1200; 1300; 1500; 1500 Cabriolet; 1600 US model.

1200 Dual braking system and steering lock added.

1500 Engine lid has twin air-intake slots added.

1600 US *model* fitted with 57bhp engine (full details under 1971 models). Enlarged front-turn signals combined with side-marker lights. Reflectors mounted on rear bumper. Side reflectors built into tail-light housing. Head restraints reduced in size. Buzzer sounds when door is opened and key is left in ignition.

1971 MODEL YEAR (begins August 1970)

Models available: 1200; 1300; 1600 (1302S) Super Beetle; 1302; 1302S Cabriolet.

1600 (1302S) Super Beetle 1500 replaced with new 1600 model ('Super Beetle') also available with 1300 engine, later known as 1302S, with 1584cc engine, compression ratio 7.5:1, developing 60bhp (SAE) at maximum 4,400rpm. New front suspension by McPherson strut, consisting of two large coil-springs, with shock-absorber mounted inside each, connected by struts to the stub-axle back-plate assemblies. Double-jointed rear axle with constant-velocity joint mounted at each end of half-axle with semi-trailing arms. Combined with new front suspension this gives marked improvement in cornering and general handling. Front hood redesigned—now larger with bulbous appearance which, combined with redesigned front suspension permits spare tyre to be repositioned horizontally instead of vertically under hood and front luggage area to be increased by 85 per cent. Seven new fresh-air outlets at windshield with direction lever allowing fresh air to be diverted from screen to interior or vice versa. Disc brakes at front.

1300 Engine output increased to 52bhp (SAE); compression ratio raised to 7.5:1 at maximum 4,100rpm. Larger front drum brakes, and improved ventilation achieved by four fresh-air inlets at windshield.

1300/1600 (1302S) Super Beetle 1302 Through-flow ventilation, expelling air through crescent-shaped louvres situated behind rear passengers' windows. Reduced lift-off distance between throttle and brake pedals.

All models Towing eyes front and rear. Larger windshield washer bottle. Headlamps re-wired to cut out automatically when ignition is switched off, leaving parking lights on.

Super Beetle US (often referred to as 'Super Bug') introduced in August 1969 with 57bhp engine, now increased to 60bhp. Larger tail lights. Two-speed fresh-air blower.

Standard Beetle (sometimes referred to as 'Custom Beetle') US *version*. First cheaper alternative model to be offered in USA with front torsion-bar suspension, smaller 1300 front hood, plain two-spoke steering wheel with centre horn push, no trim around front windshield, no floor carpeting, no electrically heated rear window and stick shift not available as optional extra.

1972 MODEL YEAR (begins August 1971)

Models available: 1200; 1300; 1302S Super Beetle; 1302; 1302S Cabriolet.

All models Plug-in computer diagnosis covering eighty-eight different fault-finding checks with computer print-out card, thus eliminating human error and providing major improvement in engine tuning. Slightly larger rear window giving 11 per cent increased visibility. Improved door handles with larger finger triggers. Improved emission control achieved by modified distributer and pre-heat air intake. Stronger anti-burst door locks.

1300/1302S New safety four-spoke non-splinter steering wheel with padded centre. Rear air extractors now fitted with draught-free one-way flaps. Combined windshield-washer wiper lever mounted on steering column. Hinged parcel shelf over back seat.

1302S Padded facia for improved safety. Improved disc brakes. New 100mph speedometer.

1200 Electrics changed from 6 to 12 volts, in line with other models.

US *1302S Super Bug* Dual braking-system warning light. Air-intake slots increased from two to four on engine lid.

1973 MODEL YEAR (begins August 1972)

Models available: 1200; 1300; 1300A; 1303; 1303S; 1303S Cabriolet; Sports Bug.

1303/1303S/1303S Cabriolet These supersede the 1302 and 1302S Super Beetle. Mechanically the same as 1302S, but with a number of improvements and new innovations. Available in two engine sizes—1584cc (as 1302S) and 1285cc, both with 52bhp engine as the 1300. Curved windshield for improved vision and slightly increased interior space, originally designed to facilitate air bags on US models which inflate on impact. Rear bumper extended by 1in. New large rear-lamp clusters incorporating tail-light flashers and reversing lights. Re-styled instrument panel with safety rocker switches. Hooded speedometer with facia finished in non-reflective padded black leatherette with built-in collapsible feature for safety. Additional heater outlets for de-frosting system, with large ventilation duct over centre of facia and direction control; improved air intake for faster warm-up.

1303S Nickel-plated anti-corrosive silencer.

1300/1303/1303S Collapsible steering column, fitted with safety, sheer-off, interior element and crash pad.

1200/1303/1303S/1303S Cabriolet More comfortable front seats with improved lateral support and range of adjustment of no less than eighty-four different positions. Gear lever and handbrake moved nearer to driving seat. Easier-action clutch. Softer transmission mountings to reduce interior noise levels. Improved gear ratios for general improvement in performance. Shorter tail pipes. Windshield wipers changed from chrome to matt black finish.

1300A A new model 1200 with 1300 engine, acting as a cheaper alternative to the 1300 without loss of performance.

1303S US model Steel bar mounted behind front bumper for added protection. Inertia safety belts. 6.00 15L tyres with $4\frac{1}{2}$in wide wheels.

Sports Bug Limited edition of 20,000 Sports Bug Beetles featuring special wheels, wide tyres, sports 'Indy' steering wheel, racing seats and racing stripes along body sides.

1974 MODEL YEAR (begins August 1973)

Models available: 1200; Jeans Beetle; 1300A; City Beetle; 1300; GT Beetle; 1303; 1303S; 1600.

1600 New 'Big Beetle' with $5\frac{1}{2}$J wheels and 175HR radial tyres, cord seat covers, full-length carpeting, leather-covered steering wheel with wooden gear knob, and imitation wood veneer on lower part of facia (available in UK). German version more luxurious with inertia seat belts, reversing lights, heated rear window etc.

UK *GT Beetle* Limited edition of 2,500 models. A special celebration Beetle to commemorate the 250,000th Beetle to enter Britain since 1953, featuring a 1300 model with 1584cc engine, plus extras, eg, front disc brakes, special wheels and cloth upholstery, also larger rear lights as fitted to 1303 and special colours.

Jeans Beetle 1200 special model with blue denim upholstery, sports steering wheel, radio, heated rear window, black bumper and black stripe along side.

City Beetle German model of 1303 with 1300 engine designed for the shopper. Special seat covers, radio, carpeting, inertia seat belts, sports wheels, heated rear window, parking-disc, pocket on sunvisor.

1200/1300/1300A (1200 with 1300 engine) Now fitted with large rear-light clusters and open-box bumpers (same as 1303).

1302S USA *Super Bug* Slightly smaller head restraints. Ignition safety device prevents car starting till safety belts are fastened. Park position for automatic stickshift. Warning light for handbrake.

1975 MODEL YEAR (begins August 1974)

Models available: 1300; 1300A; 1303; 1303S Cabriolet; 1303S Saloon discontinued.

All models Larger front direction indicators, moved from top of wing and integrated into front bumpers. (US models retain indicators on tops of wings.) Black plastic hub-caps. (US models retain chrome trims.)

Electronic voltage regulator moved from under rear seat to generator housing.

1300/1303 Stronger bumper mountings with towing eye moved from front axle to bumper.

US *Super Bug* Electronic fuel injection with 'Fuel Injection' badge on engine lid. Brake horse power increased from 46 to 48 (SAE). Clutch-pedal pressure eased. More accurate computer diagnosis. EGR light in odometer housing, notifying driver of service requirements. Californian model fitted with catalytic converter measuring approximately 4in by 10in and fitted beneath rear in front of single tail pipe. The converter raises temperature from approximately 500°F (260°C) to 1000°F (540°C), to help burn off remaining carbon-monoxide and hydro-carbons from exhaust gases. Fuel filler neck on Californian model fitted with smaller opening designed to take only fuel nozzles at gas stations selling lead-free petrol. Maintenance intervals extended to 15,000 miles (24,140km).

1976 MODEL YEAR (begins August 1975)

Models available: 1200; 1200L; 1200S; 1200LS; 1200 Auto; 1200L Auto; 1200S Auto; 1200LS Auto; (1300/1300A/1303 all discontinued).

1200L More luxurious version of 1200 with extras such as chromed bumper with rubber strips, two-speed fresh-air blower, through-flow ventilation, reclining seats, wash-wipe system with water channels built into wiper blades, padded instrument panel, reversing back-up lights, more comfortable front seats, three-spoke safety steering wheel with crash pad and sheer-off element door pocket and armrest.

1200S/1200L/1200LS 1200 with 1584cc engine with equaliser spring at rear, and front disc brakes.

1200S Auto 1200S with stick shift.

1200LS Auto 1200LS with stick shift.

All models New speedometer readings with mph on outer perimeter and kph on inner.

US '*La Grande Bug*' Luxury version of Super Bug with plusher appearance and many extras such as metallic-paint finish (choice of colours), full-carpeting, sports steering wheel, improved front seats, two-speed fresh-air blower and extra chrome trim. Auto stick shift discontinued.

1977 MODEL YEAR (begins August 1976)

Models available: 1200L; 1303LS Cabriolet.

1303LS Cabriolet Fitted with self-stabilising steering system, wide wheels and heated rear window.

1978 MODEL YEAR (begins August 1977)

1303LS Cabriolet Continues.
European Beetle No notable changes.
US *La Grande Bug* Fitted with adjustable headrest and luxury upholstery.

1979 MODEL YEAR (begins August 1978)

Beetle Ceases production in Germany.
Cabriolet Discontinued.
1200L Now imported into Germany from Mexico with four sets of engine louvres on engine lid (same as 1303). Polka-dot seat covers; no other significant changes.

INDEX

Index

205